INVENTORY 98

Twayne's Theatrical Arts Series

Warren French
EDITOR

Surrealism and American Feature Films

Albert Lewin, director's megaphone on head, with Jack Cardiff, in Spain during the shooting of the bullfight scene for *Pandora and the Flying Dutchman* (1951).

Surrealism and American Feature Films

J. H. MATTHEWS

BOSTON

Twayne Publishers

1979

**Surrealism and American
Feature Films**

is first published in 1979 by Twayne Publishers,
A Division of G. K. Hall & Co.

Copyright © 1979 by G. K. Hall & Co.

Printed on permanent / durable acid-free paper and bound
in the United States of America

First Printing, October 1979

Library of Congress Cataloging in Publication Data

Matthews, J. H.
Surrealism and American Feature Films

(Twayne's theatrical arts series)
Bibliography: p. 201-202
Includes index.
1.   Surrealism in motion pictures.
2.   Moving-pictures – United States – History.
I.   Title.
PN1995.9.S85M33   791.43 0909 1   79-4607
ISBN 0-8057-9265-1

Contents

About the Author

EDITOR of *Symposium* since 1965, J. H. Matthews is American correspondent for *Edda* and *Gradiva* (Brussels), *Phases* (Paris), and *Sud* (Marseilles). He holds two B.A. degrees from the University of Wales and a doctorate in Letters from the Université de Montpellier. In 1977 the University of Wales conferred upon him its D.Litt. for his work on Surrealism, to which he has devoted thirteen of nineteen published books. Among the reference works in which he is listed are *International Who's Who in Poetry* and *Dictionnaire général du Surréalisme*. A member of the committee appointed by the French government's Centre National de la Recherche scientifique to establish a center in Paris for documenting Surrealism worldwide, he helped the Los Angeles County Museum of Art prepare its 1974 program "The Surrealist Film." His *Surrealism and Film* (1971) was a Pulitzer Prize nominee.

Editor's Foreword

BECAUSE THE FIRST DOZEN BOOKS to be published in this series have all dealt with the careers of individual film directors, it may have appeared that we had projected a program of only rigorously *auteurist* studies. We are, therefore, particularly pleased to be able to include, as part of the expanded offering with which we launch our third year, the first of a group of books that will deal with films from various makers that illustrate international movements or tendencies in the cinema.

We do not intend to include in this series books about such prominent "genres" of motion pictures as Westerns, musicals, or horror films, as these have already been widely surveyed by competent critics and the format of our series would permit only superficial reviews of such persistent types. What we propose rather is to scrutinize intensively small groups of films representative of influential developments in the expansion of the cinema and its relationship to the arts generally. This initial study of Surrealism in the American cinema will be followed, for example, by considerations of German expressionism of the 1920s and its influences, post-World-War-II Italian neoRealism, and the "Golden Age" of French lyric cinema in the 1930s.

We are especially fortunate to have been able to enlist for the first title in this program the services of a scholar who has become an international authority on every phase of the surrealist movement. J. H. Matthews has already published more than a dozen books about Surrealism, ranging from introductory studies of its history and program to specialized accounts of its manifestation in the various arts. Especially relevant to our interests is his *Surrealism and Film* (1971), which traces the rise of the Surrealists' interest in film, the scripts and non-commercial films produced by members of the movement, and the work of Luis Buñuel, whose extraordinary achievements in creating commercial films consistent with the program of the Surrealists has already been studied in this series by Virginia Higginbotham. Some of the material from his earlier book, Matthews has outlined here in an especially comprehensive Chronology that traces the relationship of the Surrealist movement to international cinema.

The present book can, however, be read entirely independently of Matthews's earlier study; for here he investigates not any formal introduction of a Surrealist program into the United States, but rather the largely accidental appearance in American talking pictures beginning in the 1930s of elements particularly appealing to the Surrealist sensibility. Of the seven films considered, only *Pandora and the Flying Dutchman* by the outrageously neglected Albert Lewin (probably best known for his remarkable *The Picture of Dorian Gray* [1945]) was a deliberate attempt by a director familiar and sympathetic with Surrealist doctrines to employ them in the shaping of a singular picture that was, unhappily, received with the same kind of ignorance and contempt that greeted often Surrealist efforts in other arts. Five of the other six pictures, because of their unpremeditated affinities with Surrealist tastes, serve to show that the Surrealist viewpoint was not—as sometimes assumed—limited to a small group of cultists with an esoteric program.

The earliest pictures considered—the Marx Brothers' *Duck Soup* and the original *King Kong*—have long since established themselves as among the most frequently revived favorites of several generations of American filmgoers, largely because of the appeal of the same elements that originally attracted the Surrealists to them. Hopefully, Matthews's observations will win new audiences for four less known, but equally original films—*Peter Ibbetson, Dark Passage*, Charles Laughton's *The Night of the Hunter*, and Lewin's *Pandora*. This book does not simply identify Surrealist elements in these films, however; it also uses them to acquaint readers inductively with the characteristics of Surrealism—not setting these forth in a doctrinaire manner, but illustrating their existence in intriguing evidence. The American film industry may thus, paradoxically, serve to acquaint new fans with a sensibility that it has always approached with suspicious caution.

As Matthews suggests in his illuminating analysis of Marty Feldman's recent *The Last Remake of Beau Geste*, the American attitude toward Surrealism may be maturing; for, as he points out, this picture was well-financed, elaborately produced, and well-received by the public. It marks, therefore, a particularly appropriate occasion for looking back at its forerunners. Indeed one of the principal values of this book, I believe, is that it can serve as a basic text for a series of programs illustrating the progress of Surrealism in American film, using those discussed here, along with others in which readers may begin to find unexpected value.

(I would suggest, for example, as I have to the author, some of the most original works of Richard Lester—director earlier of the BBC "Goon Show," which is discussed in Matthews's *Toward the Poetics of Surrealism*—such as *Help!*, his second feature with the Beatles, and *How I Won the War*; or also such a work of Marty Feldman's sponsor Mel Brooks as *Blazing Saddles*. The reception of these pictures helps illustrate the shifting American reaction to Surrealist visions. *Help!* (1965) succeeded because of the Beatles, but clearly puzzled many who preferred the offhand realism of their preceding *A Hard Day's Night*. *How I Won the War* (1967) intimidated audiences, though it won some critical approval; but by the time of *Blazing Saddles* (1974) young Americans especially could respond to its comic non sequiturs with enthusiasm. By then, of course, many Americans had come to share as a result of the Vietnam debacle and Watergate the Surrealists' long-standing detestation of "Establishments" of any kind.)

In any event, I hope that this book will encourage the curious who have looked perplexedly on Surrealism as something remote and inscrutable to begin to see it as a liberating force in broadening responses to their own environment. I hope it will lead them to J. H. Matthews's other books and to their own explorations of the surprises that may be concealed in familiar works of art. (The major point stressed in Matthews's chapter on *Pandora and the Flying Dutchman*, for example, is that Surrealists "look at films in a way peculiarly and revealingly their own" and that they can look at the same film as a nonSurrealist and "not see the same thing at all.") As the largely

European origin of the books mentioned in the accompanying bibiography testify, a great deal remains to be done toward developing a consciousness of the Surreal in the United States.

W.F.

Preface

THIS BOOK was written under the working title *Surrealism in Hollywood* which, for reasons never explained, has been replaced. Could it be that the original title presented too challenging an anomaly? That seems quite probable. Hollywood has never ceased to equate cinema with big business enterprise, based on mass appeal. In contrast, most people think of Surrealism as identifiable with strangeness, taken to the stage of the esoteric at times. And indeed, no participant in the Surrealist movement would deny that Surrealism exercises its peculiar attraction over a relatively limited audience. It challenges and rewards minds that share assumptions, interests, curiosities, and aspirations altogether incompatible with those upon which the Hollywood film industry thrives.

While resident in Hollywood during the Second World War, the American Surrealist Man Ray wrote, in a letter to Gilbert Neiman dated October 26, 1944 (quoted here for the first time, by permission of Mrs. Carol Neiman):

I have been doing a lot of talking lately, in private and in public. Tonight I address an audience at the showing of my old films. It's not so much fun in Hollywood. They watch you as you talk, saying 'screwball' to themselves, and note carefully any leads that can be redigested into bread and margarene [*sic*]. And then again it is fun, because they feel lower than they did before, they stammer when they try to question, or become inarticulate. I feel like a million dollars when they are being modest and humble, apologetic about their own work, and in a desperate last gasp refer me to the box-office as justification, its prolongation of the sentence. Now and then some young thing with shining face, who has been secretly masturbating (it's only the old philosophers who masturbate in public, and are immediately put away), comes up to me and implores me to demonstrate my technical dexterity, to show her the way. Fortunately, she brings along her mother. It's a game of hide and seek. Or rather of seek and hide! Mothers are helpful, too.

One could not ask for clearer, more persuasive evidence of the fundamental incompatibility separating Surrealism and Hollywood commercialism.

That Surrealism should be present at all, in Hollywood, seems at first sight not only incongruous but distinctly unlikely. Yet, paying attention over the years to the medium of cinema, which has retained a special fascination for them, Surrealists have never quite turned their backs on the center of movie commercialism. They have found much to deprecate there, naturally, often deriding Hollywood practice, in fact, as irremediably epitomizing the most negative aspects of the commercial cinema and therefore as fundamentally opposed to fostering the realization of their dearest ambitions. Nevertheless, their persistence has been rewarded. They have had occasion to salute certain movies with enthusiasm. In these they have detected abiding qualities that sustain their faith in cinema as a mode of communication they have not hesitated to term poetic.

The essay that follows concentrates in the main on Hollywood films that have commanded the Surrealists' admiration. Over the years, all but one of these movies—Feldman's *The Last Remake of Beau Geste* (too recent to have done so)—have attained the status of classics in Surrealist lore. With the notable exception of Albert Lewin's *Pandora and the Flying Dutchman*, conceived and filmed in the very spirit from which Surrealism takes flight, they are examples of purely involuntary Surrealist expression through the medium of cinema. Usually, they reflect in the film-maker neither sympathy for Surrealism nor even nodding acquaintance with Surrealist ethical principles and the demands these impose on cinema. Yet each of the movies in question is distinguished by features to which a Surrealist can respond very positively. In short, for a variety of reasons these are indisputably unrepresentative examples of commercial cinema.

The Last Remake of Beau Geste calls for a special comment that no one is so well qualified to provide as its director. This book was already complete when, without knowledge of the treatment it gives his film, Marty Feldman responded to an inquiry asking simply if *The Last Remake* reflects any knowledge of and influence from Surrealism. His letter, dated December 28, 1978, reads, in part:

> I found your theories totally valid, and I've always been aware (when I was a writer, before I became an actor) of Surreal influences. I found it difficult to accept the academic totalitarianism of the Surrealist Manifesto. It seems to me too rigid and formal to embrace fully. I suppose I'm a hybrid, insofar that I'm equally influenced by Dada. Politically and creatively, I'm determinedly schizoid. I am a Marxist / Anarchist (I think this year's word is "eclectic".) It is the Surrealists who became infected with Dada that interest me most. The painter, Magritte, Tristan Tzara; Ionesco as a philosopher, but not as a playwright; early Alfred Jarry as a playwright, but *certainly* not as a philosopher.
>
> The deliberate use of Magritte-like images in my movie was an attempt to say, to paraphrase Magritte, what you see is a representation of life; it is not life. I refer you to Magritte's paintings of a pipe. This is a rather long-winded answer to your query, but I'm afraid that were I to express my thoughts and ideas on Surrealism, my letter would of needs be about four times as long as your book. . . .
>
> P.S. I noticed that some of the people that I have mentioned do not come under the classic definition of "Surrealists." I'm using my own definition. The same applies to the Dadaists. To hell with other people's definitions!

In certain significant respects running counter to customary trends in film-making, the movies examined here can be expected to make no longterm impact on Hollywood's conception of its function, of movie-making as a process for turning out marketable products with wide consumer appeal. In every instance but two, therefore, the very exceptional nature of the films under consideration results from a fortuitous combination of circumstances. In the surrealists' estimation, taking place—to their delight—quite beyond directorial supervision, the latter raises these movies above the level of mediocrity to which Surrealists see Hollywood as dedicating its efforts. Thus for the Surrealist mind it is a token of their singular value that, to a greater or lesser degree, all the motion pictures discussed here have escaped contamination by the environment that, against all expectations, somehow has produced them.

Implicit in the Surrealists' favorable reaction to selected

Hollywood feature films, of which a representative sampling is offered below, is the discovery that, occasionally anyway, the cinema is capable of satisfying demands they make of it, while still complying with the dictates of commercialism. In no small measure, then, movies of this kind generate a special kind of wonder in the Surrealist spectator: they solicit and hold his interest by accident, not design, chance having made them what they are—or, more exactly, what he finds them to be.

J.H.M.

Tully, New York

Acknowledgments

IN preparing this book as a tribute to the memory of Albert
Lewin, I incurred debts which it is a pleasure to acknowledge.

I am obligated to Alfred B. Charley and Mrs. Carol Neiman
for making available unpublished material and to Bill O'Connell for his considerate cooperation. I should like to acknowledge Marty Feldman's warm interest and to thank him and
Aurélien Dauguet for generous authorization to quote from
letters not intended for publication. To Paul Hammond I extend my gratitude for putting his shoulder to a wheel that,
without his effort, might never have turned at all. To Warren
French goes my appreciation for faith, hope, and charity; to
Siân Matthews, my affectionate thanks for insights shared
when watching films with me; to her mother, my admiration
for remaining my wife.

Chronology

*Development of the Surrealist Movement in
Relationship to International Cinema*

1919   André Breton and Philippe Soupault compose *Les Champs magnétiques*, later to be acknowledged in Surrealist circles as the first specifically Surrealist text. Both Louis Aragon and Soupault begin commenting on film in the magazine *Littérature*, cofounded by them and Breton. Among their favorite forms of cinematic expression are American slapstick comedy and serials like Louis Gasnier's *The Exploits of Elaine* and *The Perils of Pauline*. Robert Wiene directs *Das Kabinett des Dr. Caligari*.

1922   F. W. Murnau, *Nosferatu, eine Symphonie des Grauens*.

1923   In April Robert Desnos begins writing film reviews for *Paris Journal*. Benjamin Christiansen, *Haxan*. Paul Leni, *Das Wachsenfiguren Kabinett*.

1924   René Clair & Francis Picabia, *Entr'acte**. André Breton publishes his *Manifeste du surréalisme* in October, the month that Desnos begins reviewing movies for the *Journal littéraire*. The first number of *La Révolution surréaliste* appears in December.

1926   Marcel Duchamp, *Anémic Cinéma**.

1927   Desnos's film reviews begin appearing in *Le Soir*. Germaine Dulac makes *La Coquille et le clergyman* from a scenario by Antonin Artaud, falsely identified among the credits as "a dream of Antonin Artaud's." Leni, *The Cat and the Canary*. Man Ray, *Emak Bakia**.

1928   Luis Buñuel films *Un Chien andalou**, from a scenario coauthored by Salvador Dalí. René Magritte and Paul Nougé make two films (one titled *L'Espace d'une pensée**), both subsequently destroyed. Man Ray makes *L'Etoile de mer**, based on a poem by Robert Desnos. W. S. Van Dyne, *White Shadows in the South Seas.*

1929   Leni, *The Last Warning.* Roger Livet & René Magritte, *Fleurs meurtries**. Man Ray, *Le Mystère du château de dés**. André Breton publishes his *Second Manifeste du surréalisme* in which Desnos, among others, is expelled from the Surrealist group. The manifesto appears in the final issue of *La Révolution surréaliste* before separate publication the following year. Breton and Albert Valentin undertake an abortive film project, an adaptation of Barbey D'Aurevilly's story *Le Rideau cramoisi.*

1930   A new French magazine is launched: *Le Surréalisme au service de la Révolution.* Buñuel, *L'Age d'Or.* Shown for the first time on October 28, Buñuel's film provokes a riot on December 3. December 8 the Préfecture de Police demands the suppression from the film program of the phrase, "The Count of Blangis is evidently Jesus Christ." December 11 the movie is officially banned, all prints being confiscated by the police. Publication of the Surrealist manifesto occasioned by *L'Age d'Or.* Its five principal sections are (in order) by Breton, René Crevel, Paul Eluard, Aragon, and André Thirion.

1931   Jacques B. Brunius, *Voyage aux Cyclades** (scenario by the Surrealist Roger Vitrac).

1932   Tod Browning, *Freaks.* Buñuel, *Las Hurdes**. Tay Garnett, *One Way Passage.* Mervyn Leroy, *I am a Fugitive.* Jacques & Pierre Pauvert, *L'Affaire est dans le sac.* Ernest B. Schoedsack and Irving Pichel, *The Most Dangerous Game.* Joseph von Sternberg, *Blond Venus.* Jean Vigo, *Zéro de conduite.*

1933   Brunius, *Autour d'une évasion**. Leo McCarey, *Duck Soup.* Schoedsack and Merian C. Cooper, *King Kong.*

1935   Henry Hathaway, *Peter Ibbetson.* Norman McLaren's first film, *Seven Till Five**. Breton, Eluard, and Ray begin work on an unfinished film for which Breton and Eluard improvise a scenario.

1937   Brunius, *Records 37** (codirected by Jean Tarride; commentary by Desnos). Brunius, *Venezuela**. Ernst Moerman, *Mr. Fantômas**.

1938   Brunius, *Sources noires** (commentary by Desnos).

1939   Brunius, *Violons d'Ingres**.

1941   Edward Cline, *Never Give a Sucker an Even Break*, (with W. C. Fields). Sternberg, *Shanghai Gesture*.

1942   Mario Soldati, *Malombra*.

1944   Otto Preminger, *Laura*. Hans Richter, *Dreams That Money Can Buy*.

1945   John Cromwell, *The Enchanted Cottage*. Desnos dies in a concentration camp.

1946   Howard Hawks, *The Big Sky*.

1947   Claude Autant-Lara, *Le Diable au corps*. Buñuel's first commercial film, *Gran Casino*, made in Mexico. Delmer Daves, *Dark Passage*. Gherasim Luca, Gellu Naum, Virgil Teodorescu, and Trost publish in Bucharest their *Eloge de "Malombra."*

1948   Artaud dies. William Dieterle, *Portrait of Jenny*.

1949   Wilhelm Freddie and Jørgen Roos, *Refus définitif d'un baiser**. Joseph H. Lewis, *Gun Crazy*. Michel Zimbacca, *Square du Temple**.

1950   Goesta Bernard, *Lattjiomed Boccaccio*. Brunius, *Somewhere to Live**. Georges Clouzot, *Manon*. Freddie and Roos, *Spiste horisonter**.

1951   Brunius, *Brief City**. Georges Goldfayn and Jindrich Heisler, *Revue surréaliste**. Albert Lewin, *Pandora and the Flying Dutchman*. Appearance of a special Surrealist number of *L'Age du Cinéma*.

1952   Alexandre Astruc, *Le Rideau cramoisi*. Autant-Lara, *L'auberge rouge*. Jean-Louis Bédouin and Zimbacca, *L'Invention du monde** ("commentary" written and spoken by the Surrealist Benjamin Péret). Brunius, *To the Rescue*. Brunius, *Candy*. Eluard and Vitrac die.

1953   Brunius, *The Blakes Slept Here*. Kyrou publishes *Le Surréalisme et le cinéma*. Heisler and Picabia die.

1954   Brunius publishes *En Marge du cinéma français*.

1955   Charles Laughton, *The Night of the Hunter*.

1957   Benayoun publishes *Anthologie du Nonsense*. Kyrou publishes *Amour-Erotisme et cinéma*.

1958   Kyrou, *Le Palais idéal**. Kyrou, *La Déroute**. Michael Powell, *The Peeping Tom*.

1959   Georges Franju, *Les Yeux sans visage*. Marcel Mariën, *L'Imitation du cinéma**. Péret dies.

1960   Kyrou, *Porte Océane**. Kyrou, *Parfois le dimanche** (codirector Raoul Sangla).

1961   Publication of Benayoun's *Le Dessin animé après Walt Disney* and of the third volume of Artaud's *Œuvres complètes* (gathering his writings on cinema). Kyrou, *La Chevelure**. Kyrou, *Le Temps des assassins** (codirector Jean Vigne). Kyrou, *Combat de coqs** (codirector Louis Seguin).

1962   Robert Hampton (pseudonym used by Riccardo Freda), *L'Oribile Segreto del Dottor Hichcock*. Kyrou, *Les Immortelles**.

1964   Raymond Borde, *Pierre Molinier** (commentary by Breton).

1965   Kyrou, *Un honn*ête homme*. Kyrou *Bloko**.

1966   Desnos's *Cinéma* appears posthumously. Breton dies. Paulo Antonio Paranagua, *Nadja**.

1967   Brunius, Magritte, and Nougé die. Jan Švankmajer, *Historia naturae**.

1968   Duchamp dies. Aurélien Dauguet founds, in Rouen, the film club *L'Age d'Or*, the first Surrealist film club ever to exist. Švankmajer, *Byt**. Zimbacca, *Ni d'Eve ni d'Adam**.

1969   Robert Benayoun, *Paris n'existe pas*. Švankmajer, *Tichý Týden v Domě**.

1970   Collapse of the film club *L'Age d'Or*. Švankmajer, *Don Šajn**.

1971   Ludvíg Šváb, *L'Autre Chien**. Šváb, *Ott 71**. Švankmajer, *Jabberwocky**.

1972   Kyrou, *Le Moine* (from the scenario by Buñuel and J. C. Carrière—published in 1971—based on M. G. Lewis's Gothic novel *The Monk*).

1973   Švankmajer, *Ottrantský zámek**.

1974   Benayoun, *Sérieux comme le plaisir*. Paul Hammond publishes *Marvellous Méliès*.

1975   *René Magritte cinéaste** (Magritte's home movies).

1976   Man Ray and Molinier die.

1977   Marty Feldman, *The Last Remake of Beau Geste*.

Jacques Prévert dies.

1978   Hammond publishes *The Shadow and Its Shadow*.

Films thus marked are short works made mostly in France and Belgium by Surrealists and other experimental film-makers. Some of these may be rented from the Museum of Modern Art, New York, or purchased from American dealers, especially Reel Images, Monroe, Connecticut and North Hollywood, California. Feature films listed here, but not discussed at length in this book, have been of particular interest to Surrealists for reasons mentioned in the text.

1

Introduction

ECONOMIC FACTORS more than anything else have stood between the Surrealists and full realization of their aims through the medium of film. As Surrealists would interpret the situation, this means that cinema has been denied attainment of its potential, by the very circumstances that have made feasible and encouraged its development into a major industry, for so long centered in Hollywood. A remark by the Belgian Surrealist Marcel Mariën is, in this respect, a revolutionary program in itself. Commenting on the fact that, because vast funds are needed for movie production in Hollywood, film magnates are reduced to "irremediably chewing over the same monotonous little story," Mariën argues that it takes very little, really, to gain access to "a field of possibilities larger than that of all the powers of Hollywood put together." All that is needed, he contends, is to "defy the Holy Inquisition," that is to say, "not to respect the rules of the game."[1]

Mariën's claim is a bold one. It implies a plan of campaign which he would have us believe cannot fail. All the same, participants in the Surrealist movement the world over have been aware that they have never enjoyed the chance to express themselves through cinema with the freedom available to them in the medium of painting, shall we say. In large measure, adverse conditions have obliged them to look to the achievements of others—most of whom know nothing about Surrealism, what it aims to do, why, and by which means—to reflect to some extent their viewpoint on cinema. Therefore, when speaking of Surrealism and the movies, presumably we have to raise the following question first of all. What does a Surrealist look for in movies, especially in films made by people whose inspiration comes from sources outside Sur-

23

The old master of cinematic Surrealism, Luis Buñuel, demonstrates how to rape Catherine Deneuve in Belle de jour.

Courtesy of Allied Artists Picture Corporation

realism? Apparently straightforward and to the point, this question takes us to essentials less directly than it seems reasonable to suppose.

By and large, a Surrealist does not bring to cinema—more precisely, to the activity of moviegoing—perfectly clear ideas about the kinds of demands he is going to make on the film he will be watching and expects its director to meet. True, certain names (Luis Buñuel's, particularly, and Norman McLaren's) offer him guarantees on which he feels he can count without hesitation. All the same, it often happens that the motion pictures he finds most rewarding (most imaginatively stimulating, that is) afford him the pleasure of discoveries made in quite unexpected quarters.

In May of 1935 André Breton and Benjamin Péret tried to show Luis Buñuel's movie *L'Age d'Or* (1930) on the occasion of an International Surrealist Exhibition held in the Canary Islands. The Spanish censor banned its projection. Soon after, Breton was to remark in print, "This film remains up to today the only enterprise exalting love as I envisage it." Republishing these comments in his book *L'Amour fou* (1937), he added a footnote: "No longer the only one but one of the two only ones since that other prodigious film has been revealed to me, a triumph of Surrealist thought, *Peter Ibbetson*" (p. 113). And how was the revelation of *Peter Ibbetson* made to the Surrealist group in Paris? The facts are as follows. One day in 1937, trailing a woman he did not know but who had attracted him as she walked by in the street, Paul Eluard followed her into a movie house. There he found himself watching *Peter Ibbetson*, a film of which he had never heard.

Eluard's experience can hardly be called typical of the way he and other Surrealists have come by memorable discoveries in the byways of Hollywood commercialism. Yet to the Surrealist mind it stands as a fascinating instance of the salutary effect of chance, on this occasion cooperating fruitfully with the erotic impulse.

What, though, are the grounds in Surrealism for firm rejection of one movie and wholehearted approval of another? It is obvious that the content of many a film is so patently offensive to all Surrealists that they would never consent to view certain programs, under any circumstances. For instance, movies presenting the church, the army or the police in a favorable light epitomize the kind of cinema for which Surrealists everywhere can feel only extreme distaste. It goes without saying, too, that no Surrealist can condone inversion of the values expressed in Henry Hathaway's *Peter Ibbetson* (1935) as we find it in Vittorio de Sica's *Stazione Termini* (1952). Banal though this observation seems to be, it provides a point of departure for an objective examination of Surrealist preferences in film. For the Surrealist's primary concern, when watching a motion picture, is basically no different from that of the public at large. Like the latter, he is interested in what is shown and in what is told. He has come to find out what is told through what is shown and to discover what is shown by what is told. Moreover, he will react out of sympathy or antipathy to everything he witnesses. At first, in fact, his attitude appears to be very unsophisticated indeed.

Just as his prejudices are revealed openly and without delay in violent condemnation of the subject matter of one sort of movie so, fostering a way of looking at the world about him, his predispositions are no less evident in his acclaim of another, quite different type of film. As disapproval of the first demonstrates no less accurately than enthusiasm for the second, his basis for judgment gives prominence to ethical considerations over aesthetic preoccupations. This is to say that he is far more sensitive to the implications of the story told through film than to subtleties of a technical nature. We advance nowhere, really, until we appreciate that Surrealists conceive of cinema as serving a purpose that, against the background of the aesthetics of film, looks to be very limited indeed. They ask of the movie director that he show a story, in much the same way as a writer would tell one.

The Surrealists' attitude toward technique in film sets their idea of cinema at some distance from Surrealist painting and writing, in at least one important respect. As proposed in André Breton's first Surrealist manifesto of 1924, automatic writing is a method by which the potential of man's imagination can be explored without interference from the restraining influence of good taste, reason, or inculcated moral and aesthetic standards. Similarly, many of the methods implemented by Surrealist painters—*collage, frottage*, and *grattage* among them—are intended to liberate the creative imagination (Max Ernst spoke significantly of means of "forcing inspiration") and to assist the artist in attaining new subject matter, uncovered, examined, and presented by way of innovative technique.

In 1968 the Czech surrealist Jan Švankmajer won the Max Ernst Prize at the Oberhausen Festival with his movie *Historia naturae* (1967). Earlier, in France Eric Duvivier had made a film based on Ernst's *collage*-novel *La Femme 100 têtes*. Generally speaking, however, exploratory technique counts for little in the Surrealist concept of cinema. The testimony of Surrealism's most celebrated film-maker, Buñuel, is unequivocal and informative in this regard. Writing in the tenth number of the French magazine *Cahiers d'Art* (1927) about Victor Fleming's movie *The Way of All Flesh*, he conceded that technique is "a necessary quality for a film as for every work of art, indeed for an industrial product." However, he warned against believing that this quality determines the excellence of movies: "There are qualities in a film that can be of more interest than technique."

The importance of Buñuel's last assertion may be measured if we compare his 1927 statement—dating from before he completed his first Surrealist film, *Un Chien andalou* (1928)—and one he made years later, during an interview granted François Truffaut for the magazine *Arts*, where it appeared on July 21, 1955: "I detest unusual camera angles. I sometimes work out a superb and very clever shot with my cameraman: we polish everything up, we are finicky and when it comes to shooting we guffaw and destroy everything so as to shoot simply, with no camera effects." Behind this remark one senses mistrust of the pretensions of the vanguard movement (with its ambition to transform cinema into an art form) shared by all Surrealists.

In an attack on the French New Wave cinema published in the movie magazine *Positif* in 1962, Robert Benayoun condemned "the unbelievable glibness of talking about cinema solely in technical language." Subsequently, Benayoun was dismissed from his position as film critic for another Paris periodical because of his undisguised contempt for the work of one of the most popular *Nouvelle Vague* directors. The antipathy Benayoun voiced, as a Surrealist, is as old as Surrealism itself. The bias evident in French avant-garde films—where cinematic syntax is developed for its own sake, while plot is submitted to the banalities of melodramatic theater—has always revolted Surrealists. One English participant in the Surrealist movement, Paul Hammond, notes, "Gance, Dulac *et al.* strove for 'pure cinema' and 'visual music', formal researches detached from the expression of concrete reality."[2] Applicable to the work of Abel Gance and Germaine Dulac, this criticism applies just as well to Louis Delluc's or Marcel L'Herbier's.

Dulac's eagerness to walk the path taken by the French avant-garde movie-makers of the twenties helped lead her into betrayal of the screenplay furnished by Antonin Artaud, who asked his fellow Surrealists to undertake a "punitive expedition" against the film, *La Coquille et le clergyman* (1927), and its director, on the occasion of its première at the Studio des Ursulines in Paris. Recalling that André Breton dismissed Dulac's film as "only an aesthetic essay," Hammond predictably criticizes its "too stable, too rhythmic mise en scène, coupled with some mediocre acting" for having taken "the roughness, the edge" off Artaud's images (pp. 12-13).

Surrealists do not wish to see cinematographic technique become a distracting element, intervening between the spectator and the story he is following. Technical virtuosity, they are convinced, must never intrude but must be placed at the service of narrative. Hence people impressed by Jean Cocteau's movie *Le Sang d'un poète* (1930) or who identify Surrealism in film with Dulac's *La Coquille et le clergyman* are not only mistaken. They fall victim to an unfortunate tendency to misinterpret the Surrealist approach to cinema. Persuading them to associate it with strange, weird, inexplicable departures from recognizable reality, their preconceptions about Surrealism in general prevent them from recognizing in the affectation of Cocteau's technical showmanship a sure sign of narcissism that Surrealists abhor.

For Hammond, the question of Surrealist influence on the American avant-garde of the nineteen-forties and later (Maya Deren, Curtis Harrington, Kenneth Anger, Stan Brakhage, and so on) is "purely academic" and those seeking to trace it are "straining after a gnat." As Hammond sees things, the psychosexual obsessions of Anger, Harrington, and Gregory

Markopoulos "owe everything to Jean Cocteau, a lot to each other, and nothing to Buñuel." In short, Paul Hammond simply reaffirms what Robert Benayoun said in *Positif* (Fall, 1964), when condemning Jack Smith's movies as "foolish pretenses," Brakhage as "an impenitent groper," and Marie Menken as "a tourist."

If we cannot look to technique to alert us to manifestations of Surrealism in film, can we look more profitably to subject matter? Indeed we can, but only after leaving behind presuppositions that stereotype the Surrealist attitude to reality and to man's place in society. Otherwise, we fall into such confusion that, forced to discard simplified ideas born of what we imagine Surrealism must be, we end up with no clear impression of what it really is.

Essentially, Surrealists react positively to a movie because they approve its subject, what it tells. The manner of telling, involving methodological considerations, is a contributing factor, of course. It *has* to be, in a communication medium that tells by arranging pictures as well as through dialogue. All the same, dialogue and plot remain the focal point of a Surrealist's attention. His bias in favor of content is worth noting from the start. It can lead him to sympathize with or praise film-makers whose command of cinematic technique is questionable enough to invalidate their work, in the estimation of people who look upon professional competence as the *sine qua non* of real achievement in cinema. When Marcel Mariën exaggerated the technical deficiencies of his movie *L'Imitation du cinéma* (1959)—with which, naturally, lack of adequate funding, equipment, and facilities had much to do—he made a point well worth noting, if we are to grasp the relative importance of substance and method to Surrealists interested in the movie medium.

Surrealists see no special virtue in technical ineptitude, however. They are a long way indeed from believing that the best films are made by movie directors who do not know the fundamentals of their craft. And yet, for them, evidence of impoverished technique is not an impediment to enjoyment, by any means. Their attitude in this respect may seem deliberately provocative, if not viewed against the background of their unrelenting opposition to formal perfection, discernible for example in their contempt for fixed forms in verbal poetry. All Surrealists are suspicious of the confinement imposed on imaginative activity by considerations of a formal nature. Too often, they are convinced, these are erroneously viewed as essential to poetic communication. In cinema, perhaps more deeply than anywhere else, the Surrealist's abiding devotion to the expression of content—if necessary, at the expense of concern over what happens to the container—marks his ideas about the value of a medium upon which his ambitions prompt him to make special demands.

This tendency marked the Surrealist concept of cinema from the very first. Louis Aragon pointed the way with his profoundly subjective film criticism, so self-absorbed as to leave his readers, after reading it, no more enlightened than before regarding the content of the films discussed. Looking back over the evidence beginning to accumulate even before the Surrealist movement really took shape and direction, Hammond observes that for the first-generation surrealists the synthetic-critical method pioneered by Aragon was "an attempt to extract the latent dream content from the dream thoughts that make up popular cinema" (p. 6). This is to say that film no longer is "a 'closed' work, a mere object of contemplation using the limited resources of reason," because the synthetic-critical text "opens up its reading, the dialectic is set in motion, and we are on the road to surreality, the 'point of the mind' where contradiction ceases to trouble us" (p. 8).

Classic texts of Surrealist synthetic-criticism do not date exclusively from the first quarter of the twentieth century. They include the Romanian Surrealist group's tribute to the involuntary Surrealism of Mario Soldati's film *Malombra* (1942) as well as an experiment in "the irrational enlargement of a film," Joseph von Sternberg's *Shanghai Gesture* (1941), published by the Surrealists in France.[3] Concluding his presentation of the data gathered on *Shanghai Gesture*, Jean Schuster explained that the goal he shared with his Surrealist associates was implementing a modern critical attitude which he termed "objective-internal." This adjective points to the Surrealists' dismissal of impartiality as "jesuitical," on the grounds that objective criticism "clips its own wings through compromises." The gravest and most common of these, according to Schuster, consists in "rescuing certain debased subjects from disfavor on the pretext that their artistic workmanship is skillful." Thus so-called critical objectivity is, to Schuster's mind, "an attack on the security of the spirit," while real objectivity, here, "is produced spontaneously" when a number of men and women sharing certain fundamental beliefs are led to judge some spectacle or activity, "artistic or otherwise." Hence Schuster's adoption of the term "objective-internal" results from "objective-subjective opposition."

What Schuster has to say uncovers the fallacy of certain misconceptions that tend to represent Surrealism as being in radical conflict with reality.

Surrealists worth their salt do not devote themselves to widening the gap between the real and the Surreal, but to closing it. More precisely, they are dedicated to developing our sense of what actually is real. This is the force of the dictum, "The surreal is that which tends to become real," in which Breton sums up a program that draws vitality continually from the Surrealists' dearest aspirations, aiming at transformation of our sense of reality under the compelling influence of our desires. As a result, to the degree that it has the ability to educate consciousness by visual means, cinema has a capital role to play in promoting Surrealism's positive principles as well as its negative ones.

Everything hinges on the Surrealist's way of looking and on the values he prizes. Thus the depiction of reality in film engages his attention only to the extent that it conforms to criteria developed in the climate of Surrealist ideas. Jacques B. Brunius observes pertinently, "For the spectator, the mental representations provoked by the screen images tend to become one with the customary representation he has of the outside world on the basis of his perceptions."[4] Luis Buñuel agrees: "Each one charges what he sees with *affectivity*; no one sees things as they are, but as his desires and his state of soul make him see."[5] Speaking more personally, Antonin Artaud distinguishes in cinema "a virtue proper to the secret movement and the matter of the images." There is, then, in movies, something of "the unforeseen and the mysterious not to be found in the other arts." For any image, "the most arid, banal," arrives on the screen "transposed." Hence the smallest detail and the most insignificant object "take on a meaning and a life that belong to them alone," beyond "the significative value of the images themselves, beyond the thought they translate, the symbol they make up."[6]

Ado Kyrou, meanwhile, declares forthrightly, "Looking at a film I necessarily carry out an act upon this object, I transform it, then, and starting from the elements provided, I make it *my thing* so as to draw shreds of knowledge from it and to see better into myself."[7] The result can be not only revelatory but quite unfortunate. Thus, citing "from memory" the last words uttered in Mervyn Leroy's *I am a Fugitive* (1932), Kyrou reports that Paul Muni rejects society in violent terms most appealing to the Surrealist mind. Yet when we last see the character played by Muni he is, his eyes staring, a broken man, a social outcast who, asked how he manages to live these days, mutters, "I steal." A similar distortion occurs in Kyrou's version of the story told in George Sidney's *Jeanne Eagels* (1957). It becomes obvious that this film strikes him in retrospect as "sublime" because of the inaccuracy of his recollection of its theme, as summarized in *Le Surréalisme au cinéma* (p. 181) and (in exactly the same terms, we notice) in his *Amour-Erotisme et cinéma*.[8]

In the long run, however, it is the principle that matters, not the possible weaknesses of its application. Alain Joubert adopts the very same standpoint as Kyrou to explain:

Cinema has always represented for me the absolute degree of the image. . . . That one can go to a show—the movies—without a profound desire to give the evidence a shake, to interpret in *different* terms the very structures proposed, in short, to decipher the true meaning of the gestures made by the characters in action, has always seemed to me as sad as looking at a painting with the attention generally granted a fine display in a "fashion" house. Not that I look down on the pleasure brought me by the very often magnificent arrangement of windows filled with the attractions of existence, but because the eye scrutinizing them could not find therein anything but the immediate apprehension of that pleasure.[9]

It is noteworthy that Joubert unhesitatingly implies that, deciphering from a personal viewpoint whatever he sees in a movie house, he succeeds in bringing its true significance to light. This meaning, we are entitled and even encouraged to infer, has escaped the director who schooled his actors in the gestures they make.

It may seem fair to conclude from Joubert's statement that, as a Surrealist, he is more than a little inclined to arrogance, where movie-watching is concerned. Such a conclusion ceases to be negative, however, if we acknowledge the Surrealists' right to treat cinema as the occasion for a purely subjective reaction—a response to which the director's conscious motivation may contribute relatively little.

One feature is fundamental to the Surrealist's process of response and appreciation. He reserves the right to enjoy what he sees in the movie house on his own terms entirely, in his own way, and for reasons of his own. He may be characterized as unabashedly self-centered to the degree that, watching a film, he is far less concerned with the purpose behind it than with the meaning it assumes for him. Where he reacts positively, a process of annexation often occurs. From this point on, the film exists only for what it is able to show a spectator endowed with his own singular way of looking at movies. It is this fact, and not the determination to *look for* something, that conditions Surrealist receptivity to movies. Whether they like it or not, it has the effect of making film directors like Ernest B. Schoedsack and Merian C. Cooper, Delmer Daves, and Henry Hathaway (to cite names almost at random) fellows in a bed where not one of them would choose to be and where none of them is aware of lying.

A list of Hollywood films appealing to Surrealists presents a bewildering picture of eclecticism that appears to contrast sharply with the selectivity their reputation for harsh judgment, brutally formulated, would lead us to expect. Where cinema is in question, it seems, Surrealists respond haphazardly, impelled to praise or attack more by whim than by demands attributable to consistent criteria. As well as Hathaway's *Peter Ibbetson*, they are attracted to works in the same vein like Frank Lloyd's *Berkeley Square* and William Dieterle's *Portrait of Jenny*—"time-travel fantasies," to use a phrase favored by Robert Benayoun, who tried his hand at such a movie when he made *Paris n'existe pas* in 1969. Movies of this kind might persuade some observers to suppose that Surrealism merely promotes evasion in the cinema, were it not for Buñuel's *Las Hurdes* (1932), which remains the outstanding example of revolt against contingent reality by way of dispassionate reportage. At the same time, attending to the oppressive bleakness of day-to-day existence has not prevented Surrealists from responding to film comedy, even when doing so (admiring the work of Keaton, Chaplin, or W. C. Fields) has the effect of making them appear far more conformist in their views than they really are.[10]

Further expansion of a list only just begun seems likely to bring with it greater confusion, especially if one incorporates, as one ought to do, unclassifiable movies like Schoedsack and Cooper's *King Kong* (1933) which—despite its surface resemblance to the standard Hollywood film of fanciful adventure in exotic climes—surrealists find to be a fine example of the cinema's capacity to fire the imagination. Even more confusion surely threatens if account is taken of the American Man Ray's testimony, "The worst films I've ever seen, the ones that send me to sleep, contain ten or fifteen marvelous minutes. The best films I've ever seen contain ten or fifteen valid minutes." Quoting himself in an essay called *"Cinémage,"* published *L'Age du Cinéma* (1951), Ray added, "That observation, made on many occasions during my ten-year stay in Hollywood, never provoked comment there, was completely ignored or simply misunderstood."[11] Buñuel's interpretation of it, in "Cinema, Instrument of Poetry," is that in all films, good and bad, beyond and despite the movie-makers' intentions, "cinema poetry struggles to come to the surface and manifest itself" (p. 274).

Despite the obvious danger of inferring from all this that Surrealism can rear its head unpredictably just about anywhere, it is precisely where we begin to despair of making sense of Surrealism in the movies that we find we have most chance of doing so, provided we advance under the Surrealists' guidance.

The most reliable way to escape the temptation to treat Surrealists as capricious and unpredictable in their response to movies made by nonSurrealists looks like being a thorough review of the principles underlying their idea of film-making. Embarking on such an examination, we find very soon that participants in the Surrealist venture have had little inclination to theorize about cinema, and for one very significant reason. They have never been the least concerned to develop an aesthetic, in whatever medium they have adopted or explored. Where movies are in question, then, identifying fundamental Surrealist principles calls less for scrutiny of published theories, or unpublished ones, than for analysis of significant films. In practical terms, it means examining a number of movies to which Surrealists themselves have attached particular meaning. This, in turn, entails seeking to establish why those figure among the films that Surrealists have singled out as having special interest and lasting value.

Our starting point must be a statement made by Ado Kyrou in *Le Surréalisme au cinéma*: "Poetic, frenetic criticism, taking full account of the Invisible, of the mystery of a film, is the only one the necessity for which makes itself felt imperatively. The critic should start out from his fiercely personal impression, from the shock produced by the encounter between the film-object and the self-subject, to objectify hidden beauties" (p. 279). It is from this fiercely personal standpoint that Surrealism casts light on certain movies. Seen from Surrealist perspective, films take on an aura that only Surrealism can make it possible to detect.

Lamenting in his essay "Cinema, Instrument of Poetry" that mystery, "the essential element in every work of art," is generally lacking in films, Buñuel explains why he believes this is so: "Authors, directors and producers are at pains not to disturb our peace, by leaving the window open on the liberating world of poetry tightly closed. They prefer to make the screen reflect subjects which could compose the normal continuation of our daily life, to repeat a thousand times the same drama or to make us forget the painful hours of daily work. And all this naturally sanctioned by habitual morality, government, and international censorship, religion, dominated by good taste and enlivened by white humor and other prosaic imperatives of reality" (p. 274). When a Surrealist watches an example of movie commercialism, his instinct, first and last, is to rattle the window, to check how firmly it is closed. He has entered the movie house supremely well equipped to do so and fully capable of forcing locks, of letting in daylight where it has been excluded and, looking out, of seeing more than he was meant to see or even, upon occasion, something quite different.

2

The Marx Brothers:
Duck Soup (1933)

OF ALL THE TYPES of film developed or brought to perfection in Hollywood, none promises to impose on cinematic expression a tone and function less acceptable to Surrealists than the musical. As no other movie does, the musical exemplifies the American film industry's devotion to the basic principle that cinema is, essentially, once and for all, an escapist medium. It treats film as characterized exclusively by a certain number of clearly identifiable features. Enumeration of the latter places in our hands a checklist of most of the distinctive characteristics of Hollywood cinema that the Surrealist finds repellent and, by extension, holds accountable for the general failure of the movies to fulfill their promise as an exciting mode of poetic expression.

Here some preliminary clarification is needed, if we are not to be misled by the enthusiasm for film in general, and for American cinema in particular, expressed from the first by participants in the Surrealist movement.

As early as 1918 Louis Aragon, one of the founders of the Surrealist group in France, wrote, "Someone has spoken of modern magic. How better to explain that superhuman, despotic power exercised even over those who do not recognize it by such elements disparaged up to now by *people of taste*, which are the most powerful against souls least sensitive to the enchantment of film projection?"[1] In 1924 Philippe Soupault, coauthor with André Breton of the first specifically Surrealist text, *Les Champs magnétiques* (1919) published an essay called "*Le Cinéma U.S.A.*" in a movie magazine where it appeared with the following editorial note: "The American film, despised by certain 'intellectuals', has been understood by the people and the poets. It is, indeed, in the films of the

37

Harpo Marx as Pinkie, in a state of military preparedness at the door on which he hangs a "Help Wanted" sign when Freedonia needs allies.   Credit: Movie Star News

United States that cinema has appeared to us as one of the
most powerful poetic forces. Poetry, as at its birth, touches the
people directly, thanks to cinema. Let the poet Philippe
Soupault thank the American film for this miracle of modern
times."[2] Not long afterward, praising a Pearl White serial,
another first-generation Surrealist, Robert Desnos, asked,
"Who has not dreamed so clearly of discovering treasure or of
embracing his Beatrice that, upon reawakening, he did not
look involuntarily for the precious stones now disappeared
and for the beautiful eyes now gone from sight? The cinema
already began to realize those illusions of the night, a waking
dream."[3]

In an early important theoretical article dating from 1925, a
nonSurrealist, Jean Goudal, had quoted from Breton's *Manifeste du surréalisme*, published the previous October:
" 'There are', adds Mr A. Breton, 'stories to be written for
grown-ups, stories still almost fairytales'. Who will write these
tales, if not the cinema?" Goudal's ungrammatical question is
purely rhetorical. It seems to suggest that American musicals
present us with the very sort of fairytales to which movies are
best adapted, the kind most responsive to Surrealism's demands on cinema.

The paradox we face here runs deep. To dispel it, one has to
do more than recall that Surrealists were enthusiastic about
movies before the advent of sound pictures, that is, before the
musical became a practical possibility. Resolving this paradox
calls for closer scrutiny of available evidence.

Musicals purvey an hour and a half or two hours of release
from the cares of day-to-day existence. They lull the mind,
dulling the critical sense, as they divert attention to more or
less lavish production numbers for which the story line is, typically, no more than an excuse. If not always set in a never-
never land quite remote from our own, a musical's plot invariably entices us into a world where the oppressive and stultify-
ing forces confronting us daily cease to operate, temporarily at
least. Here the happy ending is postponed only so that it may
be savored when, inevitably, it arrives in time to send us all
home, well satisfied.

Musicals transport us momentarily out of the harsh realities
of survival in a world generally hostile to our deepest needs.
Thus, by presenting what it has to offer within the bland

framework of an amusing diversion, a musical is more likely to reaffirm the values of contemporary society than to discredit these and incite its audience to revolt against them. Because they present a fortunate combination of circumstances whose outcome can only be happy, musicals actually inculcate a mood of acceptance. They take responsibility for man's happiness – more especially, for the fullest realization of his dreams – out of his hands, entrusting it instead to a benign force that operates successfully against all odds. Inappropriate as it may sound, the Surrealist's distaste for the principles on which Hollywood musicals rest may be likened very seriously to his detestation of religion, which he castigates as opposing the poetic spirit of the marvelous.

It is true that musicals have left the Surrealists with a number of memorable images, with which religion cannot begin to compete. Participants in Surrealism would not disapprove of the admiration voiced by one of their number, Nora Mitrani, speaking in the first number of *Le Surréalisme, même* (1956) about "the Marilyns and other gorgeous technicolor cinema creatures who, in tight-fitting red velvet, dance, mouth and eyes half closed, distracted, in the harsh world of men" (p. 7). There is no harm, of course, in admiring "the most beautiful legs in the history of the cinema."[4] But we have to acknowledge that such delectable features lose nothing by being isolated from musicals where one finds them: they can be taken from context without loss of enjoyment. Here lies the weakness of the genre.

Musicals present numerous moments of singular imaginative freedom. Yet not one of them in its entirety enters an insistent, unequivocal plea for the kind of liberation Surrealism advocates. Indeed, it is noteworthy that the censor, so suspicious when facing movies of other kinds, seems oddly indulgent toward the erotic mood often pervading the dance sequences in musicals. A moment's reflection, however, shows that it is not a matter of indulgence at all. Rather, censors recognize that, in the musical, eroticism is safely relegated to the distant world of fancy, instead of being bound up, disruptively, with the actuality of existence. A musical can offer just a whiff of desire attained, the illusion of freedom, without really stimulating its audience to seek further fulfillment in their own lives. In short, musicals present only fantasized sex, and in a manner that turns the erotic into a palliative, instead of representing it the way Surrealists look upon it, as a truly revolutionary force in human life.

In some respects an apparently suitable outlet for the spirit of Surrealism, the musical seems, in others, altogether too limited by the very nature of its essential characteristics to serve purposes to which, in theory, it appears to be rather well adapted. Something more is needed, before a musical can take on a quality that will endow it with distinctly Surrealist value. A Marx Brothers vehicle called *Duck Soup*, released in 1933, indicates where we may look for qualities usually lacking in musicals.

While not strictly speaking a musical in the way that classics of the genre merit the title, *Duck Soup* still incorporates features typical of such films. Through its special approach to the musical, it brings to light the genre's revolutionary potential. In this way, it radically alters the relationship that musicals bear to their public, modifying their function fundamentally while seeming to perpetuate that relationship and to respect that function.

There is good reason why *Duck Soup* does this. The Marx Brothers appear in a number of movies, made under the supervision of a variety of directors. Yet there is no notable difference in the nature and quality of their performance from one film to another. It is really of little importance to them, to their approach to cinema, whether the format of their movies conforms closely or not to that of the musical. What counts, after all, is their presence on screen and the contribution this makes to the tone of the films in which they are featured. Robert Florey, who served as main director for *The Cocoanuts* (1929), was hampered by imperfect knowledge of English. Furthermore, he had to work from inside a soundproof booth lest his laughter be picked up on the sound track. Victor Heerman apparently had had enough of directing after *Animal Crackers* (1930): he turned to screen writing. Leo McCarey has admitted to wondering how he kept his sanity during the filming of *Duck Soup*.[5] It is safe to say that no Marx Brothers movie was ever a director's picture. [Editor's Note: Andrew Sarris agrees, by granting the Brothers in *The American Cinema: Directors and Directions, 1929-1968* (New York,

1968), an independent entry and commenting, that they "burrowed from within an invariably mediore mise-en-scène to burst upon the audience with their distinctively anarchic personalities," but Sarris adds also that their "limiting factor" was "their failure to achieve the degree of production control held by Chaplin throughout his career. . . . (They) often had to sit by in compliant neutrality while the most inane plot conventions were being developed" (p. 247).]

Commenting on the lack of directorial discipline evident in Marx Brothers films, Geoffrey Brown has characterized the result as "a kind of vaudeville cinema, with the brothers constantly reducing proceedings to a series of variety acts."[6] In *Duck Soup*, certainly, their disdain for the rules and conventions prescribed by the film industry enabled them to fashion a Hollywood musical into an instrument of subversion.

Of those in France whose participation in Surrealist activities is documented, Antonin Artaud was the first to give public expression to admiration for the Marx Brothers. Although by that time estranged from his former Surrealist friends, in 1932 Artaud pronounced *Animal Crackers* "an extraordinary thing," stressing the liberation through the medium of film of "a particular magic that the customary relationships of words and pictures do not usually reveal." If there is a characteristic state, "a distinct poetic degree of the mind" that may be called Surrealism, he asserted, *Animal Crackers* "shares in it to the full."[7] Hard put to define the kind of magic he had in mind, Artaud proposed, as an analogy, "certain successful surrealist poems, *if there were any*." As for the poetic quality of *Animal Crackers*, he suggested, it corresponds to the definition of humor, "if this word hadn't long ago lost its meaning of complete liberation, of tearing up all reality in the mind."

From the very first, those affiliated with the Surrealist movement in France found Hollywood silent comedies especially appealing. Writing for *Les Cahiers du Mois* in 1925, Soupault recalled a period when he used to go to the movies almost daily: "If I leave out the comedies, I can say that everything playing at that time was idiotic," he remarked. Later, in his *Les Vases communicants* (1932), Breton referred to the French cinema's "treasury of imbecility and clumsy craziness" over which one "was sure to be able to amuse oneself boisterously (unless, of course, it was a 'comic' film)" (p. 128).

Breton's prejudice against the early French cinema, in favor of Hollywood comedies, was shared by other Surrealists too. During the silent era, the achievements of the cinema in France were completely overshadowed, in their opinion, by the work of Mack Sennett, Harold Lloyd, Buster Keaton, and Charlie Chaplin.

Full discussion of the significance of the popularity of American silent comedies among Surrealists would entail reviewing the sources of their objection to the increasing aesthetic concerns that, in their eyes, marred experiments with film form being conducted in France from the twenties onward. Outlined from their point of view by Jacques Brunius in *En Marge du cinéma français* (1954), the Surrealists' opposition to French vanguard movies need not detain us. What merits attention, rather, is the value the Surrealist sensibility attaches to humor as a revolutionary disruptive force attacking society, its usages, and prejudices.

Robert Desnos affirmed in the *Journal littéraire* on December 6, 1924, "It seems that, from its very invention, cinema found perfection in the comic." Artaud commented that if the Americans want to understand the Marx Brothers' films only humorously, "so far as humor goes, never proceeding beyond the facile, comic margins of the significance of the word," this does not mean that the end of *Monkey Business* (1931) cannot be regarded as "a hymn to anarchy and complete revolt."

There is no need to quote further from Artaud's remarks about *Animal Crackers* and *Monkey Business* to bring out the essential point. Had he extended his comments to include *Duck Soup*, it would only have been with the effect of showing how seriously the Surrealists take Marx Brothers comedy.

Wherever a Surrealist comes across elements to which he gives special value in material created in complete independence of Surrealism, he imposes an interpretation for which he does not feel he must have authority in creative intent. In the role of movie spectator, he takes fullest advantage of his privilege to watch in his own way. Man Ray once invented a prismatic device that, attached to his eye-glasses, permitted him to watch—in color and abstract images—black and white movies he found boring. Doing so, he offered an extreme but revealing example of the Surrealists' devotion to a personal perspective on films.

It has been suggested that, for Surrealists, the magic of cinema is proportionate to their distance, as mere observers, from the creative process of film-making.[8] Proving that they need to be innocent of the technicalities of cinematography would be difficult, though. In any case, it would not make a real difference. The essential fact is this. Circumstance had denied Surrealists the material means to experiment extensively with the movie medium.

During a 1935 vacation, André Breton, Paul Eluard, and Man Ray started work on a film for which Breton and Eluard improvised a script. It was never completed. In 1929 Breton had worked with Albert Valentin on an adaptation of Barbey d'Aurevilly's story *Le Rideau cramoisi*. For lack of funds the project failed. Alexandre Astruc's adaptation of the same material (1952) tones down the eroticism of Barbey's tale.

Because shortage of funds has maintained the Surrealists' distance from the practicalities of film-making, the vast majority of them have been confined to the role of movie-watchers, free to concentrate on their own reaction to cinema. The mystery of the film director's craft continues to be hidden from them, while their attention centers on the echo produced in their own thoughts and feelings by whatever passes before their eyes. This being the case, we have no reason to wonder at the fascination silent comedy holds for the Surrealist imagination.

Before the advent of sound (which provoked serious debate, in Surrealist circles, about the danger that the theater might corrupt cinema), the prime feature of movie comedy was the sight gag. Much to the Surrealists' satisfaction, the Marx Brothers, who came into the movies during the sound era, never neglect an opportunity to introduce sight gags into their films. Thus, as the Surrealist sees it, they return the cinema to first principles.

In *Duck Soup*, the first time we see Harpo (who, by never speaking in any film in which he appears, demonstrates incessantly the priority of sight over language as his preferred mode of communication), he arrives on a motorcycle in response to a call for the President's car. Playing Rufus T. Firefly, new President of Freedonia, Groucho climbs into the sidecar, gives his chauffeur instructions, and is left behind when the sidecar remains by the steps outside the presidential palace, while Harpo drives the bike away. Determined to make sure the same thing does not happen again, Firefly later insists on straddling the bike and starting the motor. This time it is the bike that remains stationary, while the sidecar drives off, bearing Harpo, who is not the least surprised.

The way language relates to sight gags in *Duck Soup* presents two interesting features. First, language does not help make a situation created visually seem more acceptable to reasonable expectation. As he climbs into Harpo's sidecar for the first time, Groucho comments, "If you run out of gas, get Ethyl. If Ethyl runs out, get Mabel. Now step on it." Like the succeeding sight gag, word play opens up speculation beyond the range of consistent association. What, for instance, can Mabel do that gasoline cannot? The answer is self-evident.

Second, language intervenes only to emphasize that a sight gag has fulfilled its purpose when it has taken us by surprise, challenging presupposition and logical sequence. Thus at one point *Duck Soup* plays a variation on an effect arranged by Man Ray in his movie *Emak Bakia* (1927) where a closeup of a favorite model, Kiki, shows that we have been looking at artificial eyes: painted on her eyelids, these disappear when she opens her eyes to stare at the camera. As spies, Pinkie and Chicolini, Harpo and Chico appear at the door of Ambassador Trentino's office in Sylvania. Harpo wears a Sherlock Holmes deerstalker hat, full beard, and thick spectacles with wildly rotating spirals in place of eyeballs (these put us in mind of the optical disks in Marcel Duchamp's film *Anémic Cinéma*, made in 1925-1926). Now Chico turns his companion around and we realize we have been looking at a face mask worn on the back of Harpo's head. Chico exclaims, with pride, "We fool you good, eh?"

Harpo, of course, is never fooled for long. What if he does attempt to light a cigar from the phone receiver? When the latter fails to work, he is not at a loss. He produces a blowtorch from his pants pocket, lights up, and then extinguishes the flame with an expert puff. Everyone who has followed him from film to film must know that Harpo's pockets contain all sorts of wonders. He draws on these whenever he needs to, as when he pulls out first the leg of a dressmaker's dummy, then a horse collar, and then the matching leg, so forming a visual *collage* of scabrous significance that any Surrealist would be pleased to have created.

While Harpo never utters a word, his erotic conduct speaks volumes. His compulsive eroticism declares itself early in *Duck Soup*. After being ushered into Trentino's office, he starts to follow the female secretary back out through the door, as though hypnotized. With a promptness indicative of long practice, Chico detains him. The erotic continues to motivate Harpo's conduct to the very end. He proves his willingness to assist in holding off the besieging enemy by pressing both hands to Mrs. Teasdale's buttocks, as she tries to keep a door closed. And between whiles he demonstrates beyond a shadow of a doubt where his loyalties lie. When war is declared, attired as Paul Revere, he takes off on horseback to spread the news. While the sound track lets us hear "Ain't she sweet?" a glimpse of a woman undressing at a window is all that is needed to distract him from his purpose; or so it seems until we have the opportunity to see what his purpose really is. Soon, responding to an invitation from a second woman, he has ridden his horse upstairs in another house. Shortly thereafter, we are treated to a pan shot of footwear lined up by a bed—men's boots, women's shoes, and horseshoes. Man and mount sleep contentedly beside a lady companion, presumably (both of them?) enjoying a postcoital nap.

The farcical aspects of this sequence do not prevent Surrealists from giving it special attention. In his *Amour-Erotisme et cinéma* (1966), Ado Kyrou declares the Marx Brothers' erotomania to be "healthy sexuality" and speaks of them as reaching "the marvelous domain of poetic anarchy" and as "bringing off human miracles for which theistic mythologies would envy them" (p. 142). Harpo's way of life takes its place in the "essential disintegration of the real by poetry" with which Artaud credits him and his brothers. It may seem to be going too far, to follow Kyrou when he asks in *Le Surréalisme au cinéma* (1963) if the Marx Brothers movies are comedies, then offers this answer: "I doubt it, and I hope that one day these films will be considered realist, while X-rated films will provoke gales of laughter over their 'penetrating psychology' and through their 'flagrant truth' " (p. 99).

The fact remains that no Surrealist will fail to draw an analogy between Harpo's indifference to the call of patriotism, in *Duck Soup*, and the behavior of the hero in Luis Buñuel's *L'Age d'Or*, who abandons a political mission to answer the imperious demands of love.

It seems no easy matter to reconcile Harpo's conduct with that *cynicism* demanded of today's artist in the manifesto issued by the Surrealists, reacting to the scandal that led the police to close the Paris theater where *L'Age d'Or* was playing. But this is only because its presentation in the context of a musical of comic dimensions at first makes it appear a less aggressive gesture than it actually is. Here in fact, is the key to the subversive effect of Marx Brothers movies which, in any other format than the one these films customarily assume, would draw unwelcome attention from the censor.

In an article on Surrealism and cinema, the exDadaist Georges Ribemont-Dessaignes speaks pertinently of "that pathway where subversion insidiously bedecks itself in the colors of the comic and the laughable."[9] Surrealists are fully capable of taking comedy seriously without ceasing to be amused. Those who signed the *L'Age d'Or* manifesto ungrudgingly acknowledged "the voice of the arbitrary to be heard in some Mack Sennett comedies." All of them would agree with Jean Goudal in castigating "an outworn respect for logic" with which he associated "all the silliness that subsists in the movies."

In the presidential palace, Rufus T. Firefly lifts the phone from its cradle. "Get me headquarters. Not hindquarters—headquarters!" Later at the end of *Duck Soup*, during his military campaign against Sylvania, he orders the soldier manning the radio at Army Headquarters to clear all wires before dictating this communiqué: " 'The enemy has captured Hills 27, 28. Throw in thirteen hillbillies out of work. Last night, two snipers crept into our machine-gun nests and laid an egg. Send reinforcements immediately'. Send it off collect!' "

In *Duck Soup*, as in all the Marx Brothers films, dialogue consistently defeats the purposes of rational communication. From the standpoint of reason, dialogue appears nonconsecutive because, more often than not, it progresses by association

outside the supervision of common sense. If a word lends itself to interpretation in two ways, we can expect to be con-
fronted with the consequences of following the meaning that
conflicts with logic. When Trentino asks his spies if they have
obtained Firefly's record, Pinkie-Harpo produces a phonograph record. Exasperated, Trentino tosses it up in the air.
Harpo draws a pistol, shoots the record to smithereens, and
earns himself a cigar, awarded by Chicolini-Chico. Thus,
visually, *Duck Soup* builds repeatedly on an absurd premise
laid down by verbal nonsequitur.

The Marx Brothers are inveterate devotees of a form of word
play not generally held in high regard, the pun. They use puns
to redirect attention, to distract their audience from the commonsense sequence of exposition and dialogue, that is to say,
to show how precarious rational discourse really is. By pun-
ning, they shed light on situations from unexpected angles
deemed totally inappropriate by reason. While Groucho practices his hopscotch, Mrs. Teasdale declaims, with all the gran-
deur Margaret Dumont can bring to her role, "The eyes of the
world are upon you. Notables from every country are gathered
in your honor. This is a gala day for you!" Firefly-Groucho
replies, "Well a gal a day is enough for me. I don't think I
could handle any more."

There is no need to wonder how a Surrealist would react to
an exchange like that one. André Breton's comment in his
1924 *Manifeste du surréalisme* answers whatever questions
we may have. He declares that the forms of Surrealist language are best adapted to dialogue. This he sees as two
thoughts confronting one another and reacting to contact.
What gives originality to the mode of dialogue Breton has in
mind is this belief: "My attention, prey to a solicitation it cannot reject, treats the opposing thought as an enemy." Hence,
conversing with someone, an individual can turn that person's
thought "to account" in a reply that "distorts" it, or, more
exactly (Breton uses the verb *"dénaturer"*) "changes its nature."[10]

We shall come shortly to the reason why Firefly so frequently redirects conversations in which he is involved. First,
though, we must note how the Marx Brothers' approach to
dialogue draws us into a private universe where words are
made to do what *they* want, in defiance of pressure from con-

tingent circumstance. Thus their practice of verbal humor challenges us to be sensitive to the fundamental difference between the public and the private function of language. Without preaching esotericism or willful obscurity, Surrealists never cease to be alert to that difference. Clearly, there is common ground of agreement between the Marx Brothers and the Surrealists, when it comes to reading the following extract from *Alice in Wonderland*:

> "When *I* use a word," Humpty Dumpty said, in a rather scornful voice, "it means just what I choose it to mean—neither more nor less."
> "The question *is*," said Alice, "whether you *can* make words mean so many different things."
> "The question *is*," said Humpty Dumpty, "which is the master—that's all."

Any doubt on this score is dispelled once we listen to Chico Marx as Chicolini, accused of treason by the Freedonian government.

Chico imperturbably misconstrues words, whether by choice or accident *defusing* them, so changing a menacing situation into one that answers his own needs. At first, it seems natural to assume that, a foreigner who speaks the language badly and presumably hears it with some difficulty, Chicolini has no conscious motive in responding the way he does, being supposedly a victim of his ignorance and inadequate command of words. Yet before long his remark, "I'm going-a good!" sets all his previous answers under questioning in a new light altogether. Implicit, certainly, is evasion of the censorial supervision of reasonable language employed according to generally accepted rules and, concurrently, assertion of individual freedom through adaptation of discourse to private purposes. When Firefly, who became interested in Chicolini's case as soon as he heard the man had offered as high as eighteen dollars for someone to defend him ("This man's case moves me deeply"), describes him as "an abject figure," Chico is off and running:

CHICOLINI: "I abject!"
FIREFLY: "Chicolini, give me a number from one to ten."
CHICOLINI: "Eleven."
FIREFLY: "Right."

CHICOLINI: "Now I ask *you* one. What is it has a trunk but no key, weighs two hundred pounds, and lives in a coicus?"
PROSECUTOR: "That's irrelevant."
CHICOLINI: "A relevant? Hey, *that*'s the answer. There's a whole lot of relevants in the coicus."
TRIBUNAL MEMBER: "That sort of testimony we can eliminate."
CHICOLINI: "That's-a fine. I'll take some."
TRIBUNAL MEMBER: "You'll take *what*?"
CHICOLINI: "A limonate. A nice cool glass of limonate. Hey, boss [*to Firefly*]. I'm going-a good!" . . .
FIREFLY: "I suggest that we give him ten years in Leavenworth or eleven years in Twelveworth."
CHICOLINI: "I tell you what I'll do. I'll take five and ten in Woolworth!"

Since language is a social phenomenon, language manipulation of this kind is a token of freedom from social restraint of the sort expressed through nonsense, highly prized by the Surrealist group, one of whose members, Robert Benayoun, published in 1957 an *Anthologie du Nonsense*. The manner in which both Chico and Groucho distort language, bend it out of shape, and fashion it anew is not an isolated feature of their conduct in society. Their indifference to verbal logic has its counterpart in an attack on sentiment ruthlessly carried on by Groucho.

According to Goudal, sentimentality is "respect for logic on the plane of feelings." Thus Surrealists do not look upon rejection of sentimentality as a mere sign of adolescent defiance. Their mistrust of the theater, during the years when the silent cinema seemed to hold more promise than the stage, is testimony to this. Spokesman for his creator, Louis Aragon, the central figure in *Anicet ou le Panorama* (1921) pronounces the theater dead, "no doubt because its sole material is moralizing, the rule of all action." He adds emphatically that "our period can hardly be interested in moralizing." If this is the case, then *Duck Soup* presents us with a hero for our time.

As the movie opens, we hear Mrs. Teasdale agree to rescue Freedonia from bankruptcy only on condition that Rufus T. Firefly is installed president. Later, she informs Firefly, "I sponsored your appointment because I feel you are the most able statesman in all Freedonia." By then, however, we have learned that her real motive is sentimental: she is said to be "rather sweet on" Firefly. He, in contrast, is quite unencumbered by sentimentality of any kind:

MRS. TEASDALE: "The future of Freedonia rests on you. Promise me you'll follow in the footsteps of my husband."
FIREFLY: [*ogling the camera*] "How do you like *that*? I haven't been on the job five minutes and already she's making advances to me. "Not that I care, but where is your husband?'"
MRS. TEASDALE: "Why, he's dead."
FIREFLY: "I bet he's just using *that* as an excuse."
MRS. TEASDALE: "I was with him till the very end!"
FIREFLY: "Hm! no wonder he passed away!"
MRS. TEASDALE: "I held him in my arms and kissed him."
FIREFLY: "Oh, I see! Then it was moider! Will you marry me? Did he leave you any money? Answer the second question first."
MRS. TEASDALE: "He left me his entire fortune."
FIREFLY: "Is that so? Can't you see what I'm trying to tell you? I love you!"

Credit: *Museum of Modern Art/Film Stills Archive*

Executive Privilege: Groucho Marx as President of Freedonia.

"To thyself be true." As applied by Firefly, the morality of
Baden-Powell and the Boy Scouts is inverted. Rufus T. Firefly
displays his total devotion to the central preoccupations of his
life: money and sex. So far as power represents to this man the
opportunity to satisfy his dominant needs, his behavior conforms very closely indeed to that advocated in Surrealism, re-
jecting values prized by society at large. Firefly's conduct, indeed, reminds us of Salvador Dalí's statement, prefacing the
L'Age d'Or manifesto: "My general idea, writing the scenario
of *The Golden Age* with Buñuel, was to present the straight
and pure line of 'conduct' of a person who pursues love
through the disgraceful humanitarian and patriotic ideals and
other wretched mechanisms of reality." At all events, the manifesto indicates quite clearly what sort of interpretation Surrealists would place on Firefly's outlook: "It is only thanks to
social cowardice that anti-Eros sees the light of day, at the expense of Eros. . . . from the violence with which we see someone's amorous passion endowed we can, caring little for the
short-lived inhibitions in which his education holds him or
does not hold him, grant him something more than a symp-
tomatic role, from the revolutionary point of view."

Although presented within the frame of farce, Firefly's
eroticism is blatant and provocative. It does no good, here, to
cite the frequency with which love becomes a central theme
in conventional musicals. Firefly does not let us forget for an
instant that when he speaks of love he alludes not to sentimental attachment but to sexual intercourse. Toward the end of
Duck Soup, when the military collapse of his country seems
imminent, he sends out a radio message to all nations ("coming to you through the courtesy of the enemy"): "We're in a
mess, folks. We're in a mess. Rush to Freedonia. Three men
and one woman are trapped in a building. Send help at once.
If you can't send help, send two more women." At this
juncture, Harpo comes through the door and holds up three
fingers. Firefly hastily adds, "Make it *three* more women!"

True enough, Firefly does not appear before us exclusively
in the pose of sex-addict. But recurrent stress on his
erotomania links uninhibited sexual need with subversion. In
the world of a Hollywood musical—where human relationships tend to be idealized—he pursues his own selfish aims
with the very kind of cynicism Surrealists believe the indi-

vidual must have if he is to deal with society's demands. Firefly's cynicism is manifest, for instance, in his activities as a
politician. Chairing a council meeting, he reveals himself an
able tactician. He rules the question of taxation out of order as
new business, when it is introduced after his call for old business. Then when the question is reintroduced under new
business, he rules it "old business already." Rufus T. Firefly
plays the game of politics as only the completely unprincipled
can.

In *Duck Soup* cynicism invades the very area where, in
musicals, we should be most sure to find it absent: song. Firefly's musical statement of policy—his answer to the New Deal,
apparently—reverses the ploy of empty campaign promises. It
openly engages him to do what other elected officers do in
spite of their promises—and even more than that:

> The last man nearly ruined this place.
> He didn't know what to do with it.
> If you think this country's bad off now,
> Just wait till I get through with it.
> . . . .
> I'm strictly on the up and up,
> So everyone beware.
> If anyone's caught taking graft
> And I don't get my share,
> We stand 'em up against the wall
> And pop goes the weasel.

The threat of the last two lines is underscored by an accompanying gesture with a stick as long as a rifle. The gesture is
repeated, naturally, when the refrain recurs to indicate the fate
awaiting the husband of any woman who prefers her lover's
company.

The major production number in *Duck Soup* is prefaced by
Firefly's provocation of Trentino, who has come to make a
conciliatory move:

TRENTINO: "I'm ready to do anything to prevent this war."
FIREFLY: "It's too late. I've already paid a month's rent on the
battlefield."
VERA MARCAL: "Oh, Your Excellency, isn't there anything *I* can do?"

FIREFLY: "Yes. But I'll talk to you about *that* later."

Firefly's grand cry, "Then it's war!" is taken up as a chorus by assembled Freedonian citizens, who earlier echoed the refrain of his campaign song. What follows is a magnificent parodic anthology, drawing upon a variety of easily identifiable musical successes, including, "Oh Freedonia, now don't you cry for me. I'll be coming round the mountain with a banjo on my knee!"

Minstrel shows, folksy musicals set in "them thar hills," where we can be sure of finding homespun virtues and no-nonsense common sense—*Duck Soup* is a veritable compendium of Hollywood's ideas for amusing a passive audience by appealing to eye and ear. Where this movie explores new ground is in inviting attention from the brain too. The chorus mindlessly chanting war cries in the background, taking up the slogans Firefly throws out, embody the spirit of nationalism in its most self-assured, most aberrant form. The fatuous ugliness of the backside-wriggling dance they execute implies a comment that requires no elaboration.

"They got guns; we got guns; all God's chillen got guns." Never before *Duck Soup* did a Hollywood musical let the public hear such a musical statement. And never before would such a statement have sounded so timely in its ironic attack on the civilized world's endorsement of war mongering and aggression. Japan's invasion of Manchuria in 1931 had shown the way the world was moving. The Reichstag was fired and Hitler came to power the very year *Duck Soup* was released. 1935 was to see Mussolini's attack on Ethiopia. 1936: the outbreak of the Spanish Civil War. 1938: the Anschluss and the dismemberment of Czechoslovakia. 1939: the Second World War.

The principle of *collage*, so stimulating to the Surrealist creative imagination, finds both visual and musical application in *Duck Soup*, where it assumes a special quality. What matters is not facing the audience with a new perspective on reality, as in Surrealist pictorial *collage*, but obliging them to take note of the constituent parts of the *collage*, each separately identifiable. Thus Firefly's call for help is succeeded by a sequence incorporating newsreel clips of a swim meet, shots of a school of porpoises disporting themselves, stock shots from safari or Tarzan pictures, etc. Similarly, identifiable musical themes draw ironic force from our ability to recognize them instantly and from our realization that they appear, now, out of normal context. These visual and auditory effects have their counterpart, at the end of the film, in an assemblage of heroic elements. The latter invade its final scenes during which Firefly wears every imaginable kind of American military uniform (and a couple of nonAmerican ones, too), together with, for good measure, a Davy Crockett coonskin cap.

There are some inconsistencies in Firefly's conduct that no Surrealist can reconcile. Personal vanity, for example, seems to provoke him into leading his country to war. But by revealing his warlike spirit, *Duck Soup* makes its point and, in this respect, merits the Surrealists' attention just like Alfred Jarry's play *Ubu-Roi* (1896). For one thing is plain. *Duck Soup* separates warlike propensities from patriotism, which Surrealists consider the bane of history. After Chico has cheated Harpo into going out to seek help, Groucho, a Davy Crockett Firefly, cries, "You're a brave man. Go and break through the lines. And remember, while you're out there, risking life and limb through shot and shell, we'll be in here, thinking what a sucker *you* are!"

While his brothers knock out enemy soldiers climbing through a broken door, Groucho keeps score just as he would in a poolroom. And when Trentino is captured, "It's game!" In spite of the fact that at one moment Firefly was shooting at his own troops, victory has come at last and the traditional happy ending is assured. As he, Chicolini, and Pinkie all throw buns at Trentino, Mrs. Teasdale rises, her voice trembling with patriotic fervor, to sing the national anthem: "Hail, Hail Freedonia." This musical finale to *Duck Soup* provokes an immediate reaction from President Firefly and his associates. Turning away from Trentino, they pelt Mrs. Teasdale instead.

Duck Soup ends in contradiction of the Hollywood convention that, in musicals, punishes departures from accepted codes of behavior and rewards people whose conduct appears honorable because it confirms society in complacent assurance that its values are unassailable. Using the same ammunition that served to humiliate an enemy, the Marx Brothers ridicule a patriot. Presented within the framework of comedy, this subversive gesture passed unchallenged by the censor.

The Four Marx Brothers: (top), "All God's chillun got guns"; (bottom), Winning for Freedonia.

The freedom enjoyed by the Marx Brothers contrasts il-
luminatingly with the treatment meted out to Jean Vigo. His
movie about revolt against the discipline imposed on school-
boys by an adult world, *Zéro de conduite*, made the year before *Duck Soup*, was denied commercial distribution until
after 1945.

Even if their tenuous link with the normal world—brother
Zeppo—is ignored altogether, we have no right to take for
granted that the Marx Brothers intentionally express the spirit
of Surrealism. All the same, they practice a form of humor
that constitutes "an implicit criticism of the conventional mental mechanism." Their films use humor as "a force that extracts
a fact or a group of facts from what is taken to be normal for
them, to precipitate them into a vertiginous play of unexpected ... relationships."[11] Are these relationships also, according to Marco Ristic's definition, Surreal? There can be no
doubt about the answer Surrealists would give to this question.

3

Ernest B. Schoedsack and Merian C. Cooper: *King Kong* (1933)

THE EMPHASIS given the original *King Kong* as it opens places it unambiguously in the well-established tradition of motion pictures meant to engage audience attention and response by way of firmly underlined mystery. This movie begins with heavy-handed solicitation of curiosity of the most elementary kind. Showing a ship, the *Venture*, about to depart Hoboken Docks in the winter of 1932, outward bound on a "crazy" voyage to a destination unknown even to its captain and mate, its first sequence at once catches everybody's imagination. Hence one fact above all impresses the spectator as the plot begins to unfold. Making their bid to attract a wide movie theater audience, Ernest B. Schoedsack and Merian C. Cooper, who both produced and directed *King Kong*, used well-tried methods, well-worn ones even, applied within limits that the commercial cinema had rendered familiar to the point of banality.

There can be no doubt that, as movie-makers, Schoedsack and Cooper counted on active cooperation from an entirely willing audience. The terms on which they undertook to communicate with their public are ones they apparently felt sure everybody would accept without reluctance or objection, quite eagerly in fact. From its initial shot, *King Kong* passes before us as a typical product of the Hollywood dream factory. Presentation of Kong in a New York theater is prefaced by the words, "He was a king and a god in the world he knew but now he comes to civilization merely a captive, a show to gratify *your* curiosity." The movie's West Coast première at Grauman's Chinese Theatre on March 24, 1933 was accompanied by a stage show featuring a fifty-voice African choral

Mighty Kong appears.

ensemble and a dance troupe of Black girls performing, among other numbers, a "Dance to the Sacred Ape."

King Kong implements clichés for purposes that promise no surprises or disturbing departures from the norms of commercialism. It aims to guarantee the general public its money's worth without unduly shocking sensibilities, flouting conventions, or challenging mental and emotional attitudes. Its directors efficiently delimit the area their film will explore, indicating that we are to enter it along the reliably intriguing path of piquant curiosity.

To anyone inclined to ask about Cooper and Schoedsack's command of the film medium the answer does not seem at all elusive, during the movie's early stages. *King Kong* demonstrates competent directorial control within a well-defined framework. In fact, to the extent that its first minutes display notable originality of treatment, they do so by utilizing a simple narrative device to emphasize that control. As the action begins, we meet Carl Denham, a famous movie-maker ("There's only *one* Carl Denham!") who, in this motion picture, is about to leave for parts undisclosed to make a picture of his own. From the first, Schoedsack and Cooper offer a double perspective on the material they present.

Although it spares us the unapologetic vulgarity we associate with the tawdry genre of sex exploitation movies, *King Kong* nevertheless is indisputably an exploitive film. Its directors set out to elicit a certain kind of excitement by alluding delicately yet unequivocally to violation of sexual taboos. The central idea of the film is credited to Cooper and the popular novelist Edgar Wallace, who died in February of 1932 before he had time to make any contribution at all to the screenplay. Asked why he dreamed up *King Kong*, Cooper is said to have confided, "To thrill myself."[1] The nature of the thrill he sought takes on definition the moment he and Schoedsack begin referring implicitly to their way of handling *King Kong* by letting Denham outline plans for the film *he* wants to make.

The parallel is more than accidental, here. The first movie Cooper and Schoedsack made in collaboration, first of what they called their "natural dramas," was *Grass* (1925). It documented the nomadic existence of Bakhtiari tribes of Southern Persia, whose search for pasture for their herds compels them to migrate each summer across the Zardehkuk range. *Grass* enjoyed critical success but did not make money when released nationally, lacking stars and love interest. In an interview reported in the *New York Times* on January 4, 1931, Schoedsack commented peevishly, "Everyone seems to think that stories, to be vital, must have a love interest. A picture can't be good unless it's built around a throbbing scene between a male and a female. That's a mistake, as Cooper and I tried to show with *Grass* and *Chang* [1927]. We focus our lenses, not on silly closeups of love-sick females, but on the elemental clashes between nations and their fundamental problems, between man and nature." Now, in *King Kong*, the audience learns that Denham, who specializes in true-life adventure films, has never before used a woman in any of his movies:

DENHAM: "Holy mackerel! [*the expletive interestingly incorporates an obsolete synonym for pander or pimp*] Do you think I *want* to haul a woman around?"
WESTON: "Why then?"
DENHAM: "Because the public, bless 'em, must have a pretty face to look at. . . . I go out and sweat blood to make a swell picture and the critics and exhibitors all say [*sneering*], 'If this picture only had love interest it would have grossed twice as much.' . . . Alright, the public wants a girl and this time I'm going to give 'em what they want."

He leaves the ship in search of a suitable woman, determined, he declares, to bring one back (like an urban Frank Buck, apparently), even if he has to marry her to do so. Prowling New York, he meets up with Ann Darrow, whom hunger has reduced to apple filching. When, to his amusement, she is hesitant about leaving with him until he has made his intentions clear, he obligingly reassures her, "Now listen, Ann, I'm on the level. No—funny business."

According to Goldner and Turner, when Cooper approached Fay Wray about playing the part of Ann Darrow, he spoke of a film about "a discovery of gigantic proportions," intimating at the same time that she would be playing opposite "the tallest, darkest leading man in Hollywood"(p. 68). Miss Wray is said to have commented in 1973, "If we'd had a percentage deal we wouldn't be such nice people. We'd be rich" (p. 197). Because Carl Denham's exploitive business sense reflects the mentality of the two men who made *King Kong* (rescuing RKO-Radio Pictures from bankruptcy), no elaborate extensive apology seems needed. His straight (not funny) business is above reproach and above explanation, too. In pursuit of the great American dream, he intends to introduce a girl into his movie so as to gross more from his new production than ever before. Business is making money, and making money is a serious business: "Listen, I'm going out and make the greatest picture in the world, something that nobody's ever seen or heard of. They'll have to have a lot of new adjectives when *I* get back!" True, Denham does not succeed in making that picture after all. Even so, his adventures will have allowed Cooper and Schoedsack to produce a movie about Kong, described in the film synopsis as "an ape many times larger than a gorilla" and cited in the credits among its "players."

The criteria by which the directors of *King Kong* invite judgment of their movie soon are outlined with perfect clarity. The assumptions on which they work and the ambitions stemming from these are beyond doubt, even if they do appear tempered with an irony that Schoedsack and Cooper have managed to make some members of their public sense. They surely have made very clear indeed their absolute certainty about what they are doing. From the beginning of their film, they show themselves fully confident of their methods and of the effect these will produce in a submissive, cooperative audience. Cooper and Schoedsack uttered no protest when the studio publicity agent announced, "It's weird, wild, wonderful—the stuff for which movies are made! . . . a show sired by the spirit of P. T. Barnum . . . the strangest adventure drama this thrill-mad world has ever seen . . . a mastadonic miracle of the movies . . . an adventure that leaps beyond the frontiers of the imagination . . . the picture that out-thrills your maddest dreams."

Coauthored by Ruth Rose, Schoedsack's wife, the screenplay of *King Kong* is patently misogynist in conception and execution. The action of the film is framed between two emphatic statements. The first is an "old Arabian proverb," invented by Cooper and ascribed to the Prophet. Flashed on the screen before the movie starts, it reads, "And lo, the beast looked upon the face of beauty. And it stayed its hand from killing. And from that day it was as one dead." The second is a

Two publicity photos of scenes not in the film adapt principles of surrealist pictorial *collage* to the spirit of P. T. Barnum.

remark made by Denham, upon hearing that military aircraft have sent Kong crashing to his death from atop the Empire State Building: "It was *Beauty* killed the Beast." Mighty personification of virile power, Kong is fated to be brought low, symbolically toppled to his death, because he has had the weakness to come under a woman's spell.

In a press release issued in 1933, Cooper explained at some length:

I got to thinking about the possibility of there having been one beast, more powerful than all the others and more intelligent—one beast giving a hint, a suggestion, a prefiguration of the dawn of man.

Then the thought struck me—what would happen to this highest representative of prehistoric animal life in our materialistic, mechanistic civilization? Why not place him at the pinnacle of the tallest building, symbol in steel, stone and glass of modern man's achievement and aspiration, and pit him against modern man?

As I mulled the story over in my mind, I saw that I had conceived the climax rather than the beginning. How would *King Kong* get there? I saw that man would have to go to *King Kong*'s world first: I conceived him as impregnable to gun-fire and too huge and swift to be killed by sword at close quarters.

How, then, to capture him? I had it! Schoedsack and I had gone to remote places to make wild animal pictures. *King Kong* would be found in such a remote place—a survival of the early world—and he would be captured through a fragile and beautiful girl. There is only one thing that may undo a brute, provided the brute approximates man, and that is beauty!

It is beauty that kindles the spark of something the brute never has sensed before. He is amazed, he is subdued by this strange thing of beauty. So I decided it would be Beauty, personified by a girl, that would lead to *King Kong*'s capture and, ultimately, to his death.

In Denham misogyny surfaces when, after the *Venture* has put to sea, he chides the first mate, Driscoll (in whom Ann Darrow recognized at once a woman-hater), with being enamored of the young woman they have brought on the voyage: "I've got enough trouble without a love affair to complicate things." A moment or two before, Denham saw Ann with a small monkey, already unconsciously displaying her appeal for the primates. "Beauty and the Beast, eh?" was his comment then. Now, while Ann is below deck, tardily preparing for her first film test by picking out and donning a dress he

will identify happily as "the Beauty and the Beast costume,"
Denham remarks to Driscoll, "I've never known it fail. Some
big, hard-boiled egg gets a look at a pretty face and bingo, he
cracks up and goes sappy. You're a pretty tough guy, but if
Beauty gets you. . . . It's the idea of my picture. The Beast was
a tough guy, too. He could lick the world, but he saw Beauty
and she got him. He went soft. He forgot his wisdom and the
little fellows licked him!" When Kong has been brought back
to New York as a freak attraction, Denham urges news repor-
ters to "play up *that* angle: Kong could have stayed where he
was, but he couldn't stay away from Beauty!"

When he and Ann have escaped from Kong, Driscoll points
out that the gigantic ape is on a cliff on Skull Mountain, from
where there is no hope of dislodging him. Denham is unper-
turbed. "Yeah, but we've got something he wants," he replies,
with a meaningful glance at Ann, who hides in Driscoll's
manly chest. The exploitive element is clear, as plans are
made to use the girl as bait so that Kong can be trapped. Subsequently, back in New York, despite her misgivings Ann confides in Driscoll, as they arrive at the theater where Kong is to
be on show, "Of course, we had to come when he [Denham]
said it would help the show." The profit motive makes the
young woman, a product of her society, a willing party to
exploitation.

In *King Kong* woman is held responsible for the loss not
only of virile characteristics (unmistakably confused with the
killer instinct and symbolically identified with the phallic
rifle) but also of sexual potency: the beast is said to be as one
dead and is described as going soft. This interpretation of her
role is in open contradiction with the ersatz eroticism introduced once Ann Darrow has put on the beauty and the beast
costume, featuring a belt (allusive to the chastity belt?), cut
low in front to highlight the pubic area.

By no means confined to the period when *King Kong* was
made, Hollywood's hypocrisy with respect to matters of sex
encourages titillating suggestive refinements in this film.
These apparently escaped the attention of the censor, who
demanded a translation of the dialogue—conducted in a language invented by Ruth Rose—between the chief and the
witch doctor on Skull Island. There is a hint of bondage sex,
for instance, as Ann is tied, arms invitingly outstretched, on an

altar between two erect graven columns, each surmounted by a human skull. Joyously anticipated by the natives who have kidnapped Ann, Kong's arrival is witnessed by the theater audience, cast in the role of voyeurs. True, it would be unwise to draw too firm a distinction between the emotions of the watching movie audience and the excitement manifested by the natives of Skull Island, waiting for Kong to claim Ann as his latest "bride." All the same, we cannot discount the fact that, for the village worshippers of Kong, sacrificing Ann is part of a cult, while the theatergoer's response is unlikely, whatever else it is, to be complicated by religious fervor.

Despite all that make the first *King Kong* look dated, it still retains a special quality, easier to sense than to describe. Goldner and Turner record Cooper's boast, "I'll have women crying over him before I'm through, and the more brutal he is, the more they'll cry in the end" (p. 56). This estimate of modern woman's psychology is not at issue. Nor is Cooper's demand that Kong be "the fiercest, most brutal, monstrous damned thing that has ever been seen." I have heard a four-year-old child shout with rage at the sight of a squadron of fighters shooting at Kong until he falls to his death in a New York street. Just as it has the power to make a measurable impact on the mind of a little girl quite incapable of grasping the interpretation Cooper and Denham place on the animal's demise, so *King Kong* has survived to transcend its innate weaknesses. None hold it in higher esteem that the Surrealists, whose admiration for this film is particularly significant for anyone wishing to know how supposedly unpromising material can look, when examined in Surrealist perspective.

Considering what we know so far of *King Kong*, approval from within the Surrealist circle is strikingly unexpected. This is a movie that never questions the caste structure and racial prejudices of contemporary society, and so condones them implicitly. Aboard ship, before her capture by the inhabitants of Skull Island, Ann talks with ladylike condescension to the vessel's stereotypical Chinese cook, played by Victor Wang, so "effective as a laugh-getter," according to Goldner and Turner (p. 85), that his role was expanded during production. In the eyes of Denham and all who accompany him ashore, the villagers are no more than savages, to be held in check by the civilizing force represented by rifles, wielded in the spirit of colonialism. Denham sees the natives' religious rites, centered on the deified ape figure, as simply a spectacle worth filming as a curiosity, duly recorded on film by Cooper and Schoedsack, who for good measure also film Denham filming the scene. Susan Sontag's comment clearly applies: "The camera does not kill, so it seems to be all a bluff—like a man's fantasy of having a gun, knife, or tool between his legs. Still, there is something predatory in the act of taking a picture. To photograph people is to violate them, by seeing them as they never see themselves, by having knowledge of them they can never have. To photograph is to turn people into objects that can be symbolically possessed. To photograph someone is a sublimated murder, just as the camera is the sublimation of a gun."[2] Denham declares that every legend has its basis in truth: "I tell you there's something on that island that no white man has ever seen." Asked by the ship's captain whether he expects to photograph it, he cries, "If it's there *you bet* I'll photograph it!" Later, back in New York, Kong breaks loose from his chains of chrome steel when newsmen begin photographing Ann. "Now wait a minute, hold on!" shouts Denham, "He thinks you're attacking the girl!"

The principle of white supremacy goes unchallenged in *King Kong.* The scene witnessed by Denham and his party on Skull Island lets them see a Black maiden being prepared for sacrifice as "the bride of Kong." The inference is clear when we listen to Cooper, interviewed on NBC radio: "This powerful beast, King Kong, who never in all his life had gazed on a beautiful thing, would be strangely attracted to this pretty white girl—attracted to her, perhaps, as he might be to some frail but beautiful flower. In some manner I could bring this beast back to New York; and then the monster, thinking of this beautiful human toy. . . ." No sooner has Kong been subdued by a gas bomb, after following Ann out of the sanctuary of his jungle, than Denham is promising, "We'll give him more than chains. He's always been king of his world, but we'll teach him fear. Why, the whole world will pay to see this!" He exaggerates, of course. During the Depression years, only the very rich could possibly afford the price of admission to view Kong as "the eighth wonder of the world." Years later, however, Kong's rights were to be vindicated. When *King Kong* (made under the working title *The Eighth Wonder*) was shown at the Los Angeles County Museum of Art in February, 1974, within the framework of a program devoted to the Surrealist cinema, an unidentified person sat through the screening dressed as a gorilla.

King Kong's racial and social presuppositions, its directors' undisguised preoccupation with bringing a money-making enterprise to successful conclusion, and above all their treatment of woman as an object to be manipulated for quite dubious purposes make this appear at first a film destined to be attacked on principle by a group that has had no hesitation in condemning William Wyler's *Detective Story* (1951) and David Lean's *Brief Encounter* (1945) on moral grounds. The Surrealists' unmitigated contempt for the values of Western society, their deep-seated mistrust of the profit motive, their idealization of women, and unyielding opposition to the coercive forces that still victimize her in twentieth-century society all combine to persuade us that nothing could be more abhorrent to them than the premise on which the plot of *King Kong* is erected.

Throughout its first section, certainly, this movie mirrors a world by which Surrealists are repelled. It does so with all the greater accuracy because its producer-directors' fidelity to the values held in that world is not merely unquestioning but obviously instinctive. *King Kong* complacently records mental and social attitudes that helped incite the Surrealists to rejection and revolt, in an effort to define their aspirations by opposition to accepted modes of thought and conduct. In France, their opposition had led them in 1930 to launch a major magazine, *Le Surréalisme au service de la Révolution*, still running when Schoedsack and Cooper's film was distributed in April of 1933.

Confident of being heard without protest, the makers of *King Kong* speak most directly and most clearly to their public when delivering a message that no Surrealist can hear without feelings of disgust. Where their movie comments on itself with least ambiguity, it does so in ways that establish one fact beyond a reasonable doubt: *King Kong* was conceived and filmed in a spirit quite different from that of Surrealism. All in all, it looks to be unlikely material for Surrealist interpretation, typical, rather, of the kind of film that, in the Surrealists' opinion, has debased the medium of cinema.

Review of the characteristics of *King Kong* noted so far reveals that they almost all come to our attention during the expository stages of the movie. They culminate with Ann Darrow's capture by the inhabitants of Skull Island who propose to offer her to Kong as a gift. Plainly, Ruth Rose acted upon the advice that Goldner and Turner say she received from Cooper: "Establish everything before Kong makes his appearance so that we won't have to explain anything after that" (p. 78). By and large, the assumptions and prejudices that mark this film unfavorably as a product of American film commercialism in the nineteen-thirties take effect during the first phase of the story—up to the point where the action moves beyond the enormous wall separating the native village from the rest of the Island. The second phase begins when the enormous phallic bolt has been drawn back in its socket so that Ann can be dragged through gates set in the wall. Now she will be roped to pillars between which women are left for Kong, while he is summoned by the sound of a huge tocsin gong.

The mystery initiated back in New York reaches its resolution on an uncharted island in the Indian Ocean with the answer to the question of what lies beyond the wall. The arrival of the giant ape (trampling trees with a violent destructive efficiency that long ago ought to have leveled a pathway through the jungle) provides that answer. However, the movie's synopsis does not even hint at the change coming over *King Kong* from the moment when the "cruel features of the island god take on an expression of delight as he beholds Ann. Gently Kong releases the girl from her bonds and, sweeping her up in one giant paw, carries his 'bride' into the jungle." Following through on its mystery theme, the movie leads us into a zone beyond that prescribed by its directors' devotion to the task of developing the idea of beauty's conquest of the beast, outlined in their name by Carl Denham.

At first, we are anything but sure of the ape's intentions, once he heads away from the wall back into the primeval jungle, with Ann in his hairy fist. Does he propose to eat her, when he has reached some favorite retreat? Whatever he has in mind, it is apparent from the start that he is ready to defend his gift at all times, against a variety of uniformly aggressive prehistoric creatures. These, despite their immense size, seem no less interested in her than he. An animal defending proprietory rights, Kong conducts himself in a way more human than simian. Goldner and Turner tell us Cooper admitted that dinosaurs and pterodactyls of the Jurassic Age "were all right as menacing influences on our imaginary Skull Island, but they were clumsy and inhuman whereas apes are similar to man" (p. 146). Hence the film synopsis points to "the semi-human intelligence of the ape" as making Kong "a fit adversary" for the tyrannosaurus rex, a gigantic beast that would have found Ann, at most, just a snack. While working on the fight sequences involving Kong and the tyrannosaurus, the movie's chief technician, Willis H. O'Brien, and his first assistant, E. B. Gibson, regularly attended boxing and wrestling matches. One might have guessed it. Kong fights like a combination of boxer (more Rocky Marciano, it is true, than the classic Jack Johnson, but still blessed with a powerful right cross) and a wrestler who favors leg dives but is also master of

Alone at last!

Credit: Bill O'Connell

the flying mare. Kong's submission hold takes all-in wrestling
to new heights of unfeigned brutality, when he succeeds in
killing his enemy by tearing its jaws apart.

"Tenderly freeing Ann from the tree" in which he deposited
her so as to be unencumbered during the fight, Kong "carries
her deeper into the jungle," reports the synopsis. Symptoma-
tic of the *macho* syndrome, his tenderness toward Ann justifies his violence toward other creatures of the forest. Soon
the erotic pitch of the movie rises, though not quite to the
level originally foreseen. Seated on a ledge overlooking the
island, Kong, the synopsis details, "proceeds to a minute examination of his 'bride', tearing away much of her clothing and
intently scrutinizing and sniffing the flimsy material. When
Ann awakens from her swoon and begins screaming, he
strokes her affectionately and then sniffs at his fingertips." By
the time *King Kong* was reissued in 1938, the censorship code
enacted in 1934 had required cutting of this scene. But enough
remained to intimate what was going on and nothing important was lost by Fay Wray's refusal to be seen nude.

By this stage in the film, the relationship developed between the ape and the girl is quite evident. Earlier, one of the
shore party exclaimed in wonderment, "He must be as big as a
house!" Watching him go off, carrying Ann, a five-year-old girl
once observed, "Doesn't King Kong have a wife?" Going un-
erringly to essentials, she cried, "Oh, he's big for a husband!"

Structurally, *King Kong* passes through three distinct
phases. The first begins in the civilized New World and leads
eventually to contact with the natives of Skull Island, living in
the shadow of a great wall "built so long ago," Denham explains, "that the people who live there now have slipped back,
forgotten the higher civilization that built it." the second
phase is initiated as the action takes us beyond the wall into a
world temporally remote from ours. This second phase dominates the movie, also profoundly marking the third, which
coincides with Denham's triumphant return to New York City.

When the story takes the audience past the wall separating
us from Kong and other huge animals that belong to another
time, the movie begins to engage the Surrealist's imagination

actively. As he sees it, passing into a prehistoric world of brute instinct is like removing the barrier reason erects in the mind and plunging behind it into a universe of unrestrained emotion. At this stage, rational considerations cease to curb imagination's activity.

Of course, Merian Cooper made it quite clear that he had no ambition to bring a credible story to the screen when he conceived *King Kong*. "In fact," Goldner and Turner quote him as saying, "I couldn't imagine anything more implausible" (p. 146). Implausibility, though, is not the aim but the effect achieved in the movie. And it is no secret that, once their film was under way, Cooper and Schoedsack relied on pacing to divert everyone's attention from embarrassing questions to which neither the screenplay by James A. Creelman and Ruth Rose nor the action visible on screen provides commonsense answers. The ridiculous disproportion in size, evident as soon as one looks at Kong next to Ann, places practical limitations on their relationship. While, mercifully, copulation promises to be impossible, we find ourselves encouraged to indulge sexual fantasy to the fullest, in the realm to which *King Kong* has transported us. Reasonable objections are powerless, now, to halt imaginative speculation of the kind that, after all, has haunted the mind of man (not to say woman) from time immemorial.[3]

The first time Ann catches sight of Kong, she stops screaming and stares. Is it her eyes she cannot believe, or her luck? We notice that after Kong has shown more than impressive dexterity for a beast of his size, in releasing her right arm from the rope binding it to the altar pillar, Ann herself quickly releases her left hand. Then she makes no attempt to escape, but drops in front of him to be picked up in one of his paws.

That Ann and Kong form a remarkably incongruous bridal couple is a fundamental departure from plausibility in *King Kong*. Our curiosity goes unsatisfied, even later on in Ruth Rose's screenplay for *Son of Kong* (1933) where Denham, seeing Kong's offspring for the first time, exclaims in surprise, "I didn't know old Kong had a son!" Coincidentally, *King Kong* confronts us with numerous minor inconsistencies that we have no way of reconciling with good sense.

At this point, it ceases to matter to the Surrealist spectator whether effects he finds imaginatively stimulating appear by design in *King Kong* or by some admirable accident. Indeed, so far as he is concerned, pleasure is only increased by the presence of certain flagrantly implausible elements testifying to haste or negligence on the film-makers' part. Far from detracting from the appeal he finds in the movie, these increase its attractiveness, not only during the sequence set behind the great wall but subsequently, too, when the movie has brought the action back to the familiar world of the North American continent.

It may seem presumptuous to infer that, later in their movie, Schoedsack and Cooper somehow have lost the control so confidently exercised at the beginning. After all, their reliance on pacing (to say nothing of the music contributed by Max Steiner) to distract the public from plot weaknesses reveals their awareness of the risks they are running in telling their story. They realize only too well, for instance, that an alert moviegoer will be able to detect one thing for sure: Kong varies in size from time to time, increasing in stature when showing him particularly large intensifies the drama of a given situation. But even in such circumstances reason is confounded by inexplicable contradictions. As he wreaks havoc in the New York streets, Kong (scaled up in size, so as not to be dwarfed by the urban landscape) holds Ann in his right hand, large enough, as in the past, to encircle her torso. Still carrying the young woman in his right, he wrecks an elevated train with his left hand, unaccountably big enough to lift one of the coaches right off the track.

By and large, in *King Kong* dramatic effect not consistency seems to have governed the use of animated models created by the staff working under O'Brien's supervision. Thus, for example, the audience's reasonable estimate of the proportions of the stegosaurus (which, in the film, actually combines features of two stegosaurs, the stegosaurus ungulatus and the kentrosaurus, from which it takes its spectacular tail) proves to be woefully inadequate when, after its death, Denham leads the sailors past its recumbent body, literally pacing out its length. Commenting on the encounter with the stegosaur, Jean Lévy has stressed the effect of confused perspective in its filming: "The first prehistoric monster shot down, for example, sweeps away the hunters with its tail, and a goodly number of the audience too." What matters here is not Lévy's exaggeration but his following declaration: "None of all this, by the way, worries me one bit."[4]

Speaking as a Surrealist, Lévy makes his case by understating it. Like his reference to dubbing as being "magnificently botched" in the version of *King Kong* distributed in France, his careful enumeration of several absurdities upon which the plot of the film is built is neither an attack on the movie nor an emotional or sentimental defense of it. In fact, Lévy is convinced that their presence contributes in no small measure to making *King Kong* "a poetic film." What is more, he sees weighty additional evidence in the fact that the action of the movie closely resembles a dream, at moments even a nightmare.

Oneiric elements are implied in the basic situation from which Schoedsack and Cooper's movie gathers momentum. As the pace increases, so these elements become more explicit, often growing out of improbabilities noticeable in the screenplay. The unusually numerous crew of the *Venture* may have been able to remove Kong's unconscious body from the beach on Skull Island. But transporting the monster all the way back to New York surely would have presented an insuperable problem, once he had regained his senses. Perhaps Denham has reason to feel well content when he boasts to Ann, in the wings of the theater where Kong is to be on show, "We've knocked some of the fight out of him since *you* saw him." In fact, the process may explain why, when we see Kong from now on, he appears to have enjoyed the benefits of cosmetic dentistry (but performed by whom, and under what conditions?). It still does not persuade us that preparing Kong for display, spreadeagled on stage in an upright position, was a task easy enough for its successful accomplishment to seem quite feasible.

The unanswered questions facing us in the film aggravate reason. At the same time—and this is important to Surrealists—they stimulate imaginative speculation, giving *King Kong* an aura of wonder, generated by all that is inexplicable here. Everything leads up to the climactic mystery of this improbable drama: how does Kong find Ann in the multistory

New York hotel across the street from the theater? Climbing up the outside of the building, he soon is peering through the window of a room that Ann and Driscoll have reached with miraculous speed. In a moment, he has reached in to drag across the room a bed (locus of dreaming and sexual encounter) on which Ann lies in terror. We notice that, although Ann is not to marry Driscoll until the following day, she occupies a double bed.

Originally the movie showed Kong pulling another woman from her bed, examining her, discovering she was not Ann Darrow (the actress playing the part was Sandra Shaw, future bride of Gary Cooper), and dropping her to her death in the street below. By requiring suppression of this sequence, thought to be too brutal when *King Kong* was reissued, the Hays Office unwittingly contributed to the wonder released in us by Kong's uncanny ability to find Ann without delay or mistake. Naturally, cutting the scene of the second woman's death also shortened the time available to Ann and Driscoll for getting up to her room, so making their presence there all the more surprising when Kong's face appears at the window.

When the action of *King Kong* brings us back to the United States, it does not break with the atmosphere characterizing events on Skull Island. If any change of tone is noticeable, this is perceptible only because the movie at last makes explicit things it merely implied earlier on. The revolting snakelike form of the elasmosauraus, slithering suggestively up from the steaming pool in the cave at the base of Skull Mountain and rearing up the rock face to get at Ann, is at one and the same time a creature of nightmare and sexual fantasy. For the elasmosaurus in the film is more slender than the creature known to paleontologists. Its swimming limbs are less prominent, making it look more like a sea serpent. While Kong is occupied destroying the rescue party who took after him when he carried Ann away, Driscoll finds refuge by withdrawing to the womblike safety of a hollow in the rock face, overhung by a bush. When Kong reaches down to probe the cave, Driscoll stabs at the ape's fingers with his seaknife and his refuge brings to mind the *vagina dentata*. Now Driscoll almost falls victim to a lizard (substituted for the spider featured in the original test reel). More than a little evocative of a spermatozoon in shape, this creature wriggles up a liana to explore his cave. Driscoll has had to climb down a creeper to enter his hiding place and will climb up it again when the tyrannosaurus has claimed Kong's attention. Later, he and Ann will escape from the giant ape by climbing down another vine and dropping from it to the welcoming water below.

How much of the paraphernalia of myth and sexual symbolism appearing in *King Kong* is used intentionally? Answering this question is of little consequence to the Surrealist. Lévy's interpretation of the film as poetic rests squarely on his belief that it attains the level of poetry in spite of its producer-directors' determination to offer "a fairground attraction on a grand scale." Whether this is unfair to Cooper and Schoedsack is not relevant. What matters to the imagination is less the intention than the results achieved. And these, every Surrealist will agree, are never more fascinating in *King Kong* than where they depart from the theme its directors set out to illustrate.

The effect seems all the more striking if one considers how self-consciously Schoedsack and Cooper stated their purpose early on, and with sufficient emphasis to leave no doubt about their ambitions. Reflected in the self-assurance of their spokesman, Denham, their self-awareness does not accurately project what this movie finally realizes. Hence one arresting feature of *King Kong*: crediting Schoedsack and Cooper with a dual perspective on their material fails to exhaust its meaning, foreseeing and exploiting its full potential. Watching this film we become most aware of irony from the moment we see its directors begin doing something other than they have told us they wish to do. *King Kong* actually contradicts some of the ideas it was made to illustrate. One of these, in fact, is disproved no less than twice.

Ann's beauty does not emasculate Kong but provokes him to display incredible strength, first in destroying the village on Skull Island and then in terrorizing New York City. It is easy to see why his conduct should have been allowed to deny the argument advanced by Denham. The sight of the great ape on the rampage is a spectacular demonstration of his awesome power and violent disposition. Indeed, after *King Kong* had been edited, Cooper insisted on adding extra footage: he and

O'Brien went on to stage the scene of the wreck of the elevated train.

From the moment *King Kong* was conceived, Cooper's thinking betrayed a taste for spectacle. The climactic confrontation between ape and modern man can be seen as having been worked out predictably in his mind, if we remember that Cooper was a wartime pilot who later flew as a mercenary during Poland's war with Russia. Close-shots of the pilots and gunners of the fighter squadron, dispatched to rid New York of the menace of Kong, reveal that the flight commander is played by Cooper, with Schoedsack as his observer. They were cast in those roles, Goldner and Turner report, after Cooper had remarked, "We should kill the sonofabitch ourselves" (p. 173). Given his experience in wartime France and Poland, it may seem surprising that Cooper allowed fighter planes in his movie to machine-gun a target (one they have considerable difficulty hitting, as it turns out) above a city, at

Driscoll rescues Ann Darrow. *Credit: Movie Star News*

the risk of decimating the population. But use of military power obviously seemed as natural to him as it is obscene to a Surrealist: Cooper, after all, was to end up as a brigadier general.

Kong's death presents two noteworthy aspects. First, he is careful to lay Ann down on the roof of the Empire State Building. The tenderness evident in this gesture is hard to reconcile with Cooper's statement that the ape looks upon the young woman as merely a toy. Demonstrating his concern for her, he sacrifices himself, leaving himself vulnerable to the bullets that weaken him so much he falls to the pavement. Second, when Kong at last lies dead in the street, Denham flatly contradicts the police captain's factually true statement, "Well, Mr. Denham, the airplanes got 'im."—"Oh, no!" cries Denham, "It wasn't the airplanes. It was *Beauty* killed the Beast."

To the very end, *King Kong* asserts a message it really has not conveyed at all. More important, in denying what they actually have shown, Schoedsack and Cooper let us surmise that, willingly or unwillingly, they have produced a film that undermines its own thesis. For this very reason, they have made a movie to which Surrealists attach special value. By the time Kong is dead, it is evident that the beauty and the beast theme has ceased to develop strictly under the film directors' control. In the Surrealists' estimation, doing something other than intended, Schoedsack and Cooper have done far more. To grasp what is involved here, one can do no better than refer to André Breton's first Surrealist manifesto. After criticizing the realist attitude toward literature, at one point in his 1924 text Breton attacks the pretensions of writers who presume to analyze the psychology of their invented characters. Here he states categorically, apropos of people in Stendhal's novels, "Where we find them really is where Stendhal has lost them."[5]

To Surrealists, the discrepancy between purpose and achievement becomes most noticeable in *King Kong* at the very moment when, against the evidence, Denham arrogantly affirms that events have borne out his theory regarding beauty's destructive influence on the beast. Here *King Kong*'s value is not to be estimated, Surrealists believe, simply on the basis of its directors' declared aim to create a spectacular entertainment. The Surrealist sensibility highlights the film's potential for satisfying some of the most cherished demands they impose on the medium of cinema. Specifically, Surrealists can detect in *King Kong* a subversive substructure at variance with the theme Cooper and Schoedsack are devoted to elaborating.

Kong is dead because society's instinct for self-preservation has resulted in military retaliation. The "final solution" to the Kong question is provided by fighter aircraft; not, though, before he has defended himself against attack, sending one plane crashing to the ground. Interestingly, Kong has taken refuge at the top of New York's highest building only after leaving his mark on the city. And he fills his destructive role during the additional sequences demanded by Cooper after the film was edited.

Surrealists look upon civilization, so called, as a coercive force, and are bound to notice that, in *King Kong*, one of its repressive agents, a policeman, expresses smug satisfaction at the achievement of another, the military. Meanwhile, especially during the scene in which he takes an elevated train apart, Kong emerges as a disruptive counter-force. His final confrontation with representatives of society's might is given particular stress by the motive lying behind his destructive rampage through New York.

Now the inexplicable emerges as testimony to the triumph of love, one of Surrealism's most potent myths, the sublime love anthologized by Benjamin Péret, the mad love to which Breton devoted one of his most impassioned books. Seen from the perspective imposed by fundamental Surrealist beliefs, love—an antisocial force that society opposes adamantly—asserts its rights in the face of civilization. In an environment as alien to him as it is hostile, Kong succeeds in finding his way to Ann Darrow. Having regained possession of her, he next cuts a swath of destruction through the city as he heads for the sanctuary of its highest building. His awesome gesture of defiance, misunderstood and misinterpreted, leaves him in tragic isolation, denied in the end the comfort of reciprocal love.

Henry Hathaway: *Peter Ibbetson* (1935)

TIME AND AGAIN, Surrealists have taken care to stress that film technique interests them only on a very limited scale, so far as it ensures the efficiency of cinema as a mode of narrative communication. Citing a few movies, among them Tay Garnett's *One Way Passage* (1932) and Henry Hathaway's *Peter Ibbetson* (1935), Ado Kyrou concedes in his *Amour-Érotisme et cinéma* (1966) that they would lack their "heart-rending power" if it were not for the "means placed at their service"—montage, superimpression, simultaneity, and so on. All the same, he emphasizes that he has no intention of pausing to analyze methods, for all technical means, to him, "are of interest only with regard to the content expressed" (p. 17). Kyrou's position is consistent with what we know of the Surrealists' preoccupation with the film-maker's ethical responsibilities. In addition, it helps direct attention to a fundamental question about the function reserved for film in Surrealism.

If we turn from motion pictures based on entirely original material to look at those adapted from novels or short stories—concentrating at this point on movies that stay faithful to their fictional sources—we need to answer the following question. Does communication through the medium of cinema provide the Surrealist with more imaginative stimulation than he could have derived from reading the text on which this or that movie is based?

Obviously, this question can be raised, in general terms, only if we disregard films in which the relative quality of the source material and its screen adaptation calls for assessment. The screenplay written by Jean Aurenche and Pierre Bost gives Claude Autant-Lara's film *Le Diable au corps* (1947) a point of departure far more acceptable to Surrealists than the

81

A *Peter Ibbetson* montage, showing the players, technicians and director Henry Hathaway.

1923 novel on which it was based, by a protégé of Jean Cocteau's, Raymond Radiguet. In *Le Surréalisme au cinéma* (1963) Kyrou has special praise for "the most cinematographic of all great modern authors": Gaston Leroux (p. 90). Kyrou, however, tends to give novelistic sources less than their due, when evaluating screen adaptations. In *Amour-Erotisme et cinéma*, for instance, he refers to the movie *The Moon and Sixpence* (1942) as Albert Lewin's biography of Gauguin, even though as Lewin's honest retention of its title indicates, the fictional transposition is Somerset Maugham's.

Nevertheless, Kyrou seems to point the way to an answer, as he reviews the emergence of the movies as a popular medium. The cinema, he argues, was "more dangerous than the written word, which, limited in its expansion, necessitates an imaginative effort." One can agree readily enough that the public at large treats written texts as "what So and So has said or thought," while the cinema as popular spectacle remains, so far as they are concerned, "unsigned." Any film (the examples Kyrou offers are Méliès's version of *Cinderella* and Hathaway's *Peter Ibbetson*) "stand on the same plane as a newsreel" (p. 19). Even so, one can hardly dismiss the problem before us by placing Surrealists among the general public, who ask only to be amused, without shouldering the burden of making an effort on their own behalf. For in their struggle against oppressive forces on all sides, the Surrealists' chief weapon is imagination.

Jacques Brunius now holds out a piece of the puzzle. At the end of his *En Marge du cinéma français* (1954) there is an allusion to the mystery of cinematic creation that, because of the richness of the cinema's means of expression, at times leads film directors to accomplish more than they intend, or in any event something palpably different. However, it is still Kyrou who assists us most, when he talks in *Le Surréalisme au cinéma* of "the shock" produced by the encounter between what he terms "the film-object" and "the self-subject" (p. 279).

To anyone who bothers to compare this movie with the novel of the same name it is evident that Luis Buñuel's *Le Journal d'une femme de chambre* (1964) is not Octave Mirbeau's, any more than his *Belle de jour* (1966) is Joseph Kessel's. But the way a Surrealist film-maker exercises his privilege to modify borrowed material is not our main concern. More worthy of note is the fact that Henry Hathaway's *Peter Ibbetson* receives warm praise in André Breton's *L'Amour fou* (1937) as "a prodigious film." Meanwhile, the George du Maurier novel from which it derives goes unmentioned even though, fifty pages later, Breton is willing enough to cite both a novel by Mary Webb and another by David Garnett, which he pronounces "remarkable." There is no evidence that, after seeing Hathaway's version, Surrealists went back eagerly to du Maurier's book or recommended that other people do so. Admittedly, Ado Kyrou complains in *Amour-Erotisme et cinéma* that the novel is encumbered by a long and pointless first section. But that is not what matters. The movie version of *Peter Ibbetson* has not superseded du Maurier's text in the Surrealists' affections; it simply has rendered acquaintance with the book superfluous.

The interesting thing here remains the question of the relative value of films and the novels that have inspired them. In this connection, Kyrou's statement in *Le Surréalisme au cinéma* sounds distinctly confusing: "With the exception of a few Surrealist books, I don't believe that love has ever had greater strength to transmute and go further than in *Peter Ibbetson* or *White Shadows in the South Seas*" (p. 125). No less disconcerting is a suggestion appearing on the very last page of *Amour-Erotisme et cinéma*: "Hold the hand of a girl during a showing of (examples [*sic*] chosen at random) *Peter Ibbetson*: you will be permitted no more doubt about what is going on inside her, about her desire to realize her dreams. Only reading a poem together can be a touchstone to the same degree" (p. 308). Even if, with *Peter Ibbetson*, we feel we can take on trust the Surrealists' disaffection for the novel from which it comes, we still may wonder what special value films might have over written texts, especially when so much evidence is available to prove that Surrealists customarily give precedence to what a movie *says* over the way it tells its story, and hence tend to look upon movie-watching as roughly the equivalent of reading.

André Breton guides us authoritatively in a celebrated essay, *"Comme dans un bois,"* first published in the Surrealism issue of *L'Age du Cinéma* (1951). Here he speaks of looking to cinema for "lyrical substance demanding to be gathered in mass and by chance." The valuable feature of cinema, he goes on to explain, is "its *power to disorient.*" Hence "the *marvel,*" next to which the merits of any given film count for little, lies in "the faculty devolving to anyone at all to abstract himself from his own life when the fancy takes him," as soon as he enters a movie theater. From the moment he has taken his seat to the moment "he slips into the fiction unfolding before his eyes," he passes through "a critical point as captivating and difficult to pin down as that which joins the waking state to dreaming (even books and plays are incomparably slower to produce the click)." According to Breton, then, the basic difference between films and books is not so much a matter of degree or intensity of effect but speed of assimilation—even where "the greatest possible intentional discordance" can be observed between "the 'lesson' the film claims to give" and "the natural bent of the person receiving it."

Breton considers it appropriate to refer to cinema as a means of expression "more than any other called upon to promote 'true life'." And he has his reasons for doing so: "What is most specific in cinematic means," he contends, "is obviously the capacity to render the powers of love concrete." These powers, he goes on to suggest, remain deficient in books because nothing in the latter can "render the seductiveness or distress of a glance, or a certain priceless vertigo." Noting how ineffectual the plastic arts are in communicating, for instance, "the dazzling image of a kiss," Breton now asserts that cinema stands alone in "extending its empire that far" and declares that "this would suffice amply to sanction it." He concludes, "In this respect, what an incomparable wake, forever sparkling, is left in our memory by movies like *Ah! le beau voyage* or *Peter Ibbetson* and how the crowning chances of life filter through under the ray of light they cast!"

Film's capacity to bring directly to our notice proof of a kind that reading and looking at pictures are inadequate to provide is illustrated in a movie we have heard mentioned on several occasions already. Henry Hathaway's *Peter Ibbetson* is a film in which it is fair to say—paraphrasing, in the interest of clarity, a remark from Breton's *L'Amour fou*—that Surrealist thought triumphs. This fact is all the more noteworthy because surrealists regard Hathaway as a film-maker of proven mediocrity, guilty of having directed *Lives of a Bengal Lancer* in 1935.[1]

Whatever reservations du Maurier's novel may call forth in a Surrealist reader, it nevertheless is an example of the "almost fairytales" for which the first Surrealist manifesto appealed. Remembered in the *Concise Cambridge History of English Literature*, next to John Leech, John Tenniel, Charles Keene, and Linley Sambourne, as an artist whose black-and-white drawings adorned *Punch* in the nineteenth century, George du Maurier must be given credit for having devised a story that any Surrealist could congratulate himself on having written. Transposed to the screen, it tells of a widowed English woman living near Paris on property left her by her late husband. Her only child, Pierre, has a playmate in Mimsey, daughter of neighbors who give the little six-year-old boy a home, after his mother's death. In love by the time an uncle arrives to take Pierre to England, the children swear never to forget one another.

Twenty years later, the boy, his first name Anglicized, has adopted his mother's maiden name. Still remembering Mimsey, on a trip to France he visits her old home. He finds the house empty, the garden where they played overgrown with weeds. While in Paris, where he has given up hope of finding trace of Mimsey, he receives a message calling him back to England to supervise the reconstruction of stables for the Duke of Towers. On the Towers estate, he feels himself irresistibly attracted to the duke's young wife, Mary, just as she is drawn to him. Each discovers final proof of the other's identity the day Peter Ibbetson relates a recent dream—a dream Mary too has had.

The essential part played by this shared dream in advancing the plot can escape no one's attention. Events now promise to diverge from what the Surrealist Jehan Mayoux once called "vulgar realism," implausibility having intervened no less directly in Hathaway's movie than in du Maurier's novel. At the moment when a dream intrudes to bring Peter and Mary together once and for all, Surrealists begin to sense that *Peter Ibbetson* is indeed, as Kyrou affirms in *Amour-Erotisme et cinéma*, "one of those rare poisonous plants appearing all of a

sudden without anyone being able to explain how" (p. 230).
The important factor is this. A Surrealist does not look upon
the intrusion of dream as setting *Peter Ibbetson* on the path to
escapism, but as marking a stage of revolutionary significance
in the lives of its principal characters.

Reviewing Peter's life of frustration up to the moment when
he dares to recount one of his dreams and discovers he already
shares it with Mary, we recognize how critically important is
this dream. We have no trouble, now, comprehending Henri
Pastoureau's observation, "Dreaming has its source in everyday life and in the imperfection of the human condition."[2]
There is no doubt, in fact, about the interpretation Surrealists
place on the dream Peter and Mary find they have in common:
"It is clear, our fate is played out between action and dream,"
asserts Gui Rosey.[3] For dreaming, another Surrealist affirms,
"has this in common with poetry that it tears the real open,"
both dream and poetry "resting on memories and the future,
irreplaceable images."[4]

To the objection that they are guilty of preaching evasion the
Surrealists have their answer all prepared. Rosey declares that
it is false to claim "one seeks to enjoy life fully as it seems to
be; one does not want, either, to create an existence for oneself
in the faithful image of a dream. Happiness would appear to
be, rather, an intermediary state." Kyrou agrees. Referring in
Amour-Erotisme et cinéma to the dream Peter and Mary have
in common, he argues, "This is not the transformation of life
into dream, but the transformation of dream into life." For this
reason, he momentarily deems it permissible to break his own
rule and comments briefly on cinematic technique in *Peter
Ibbetson*. He pronounces the style of the film worthy of its
theme, pointing out, "No fuzziness or superimposition forms a
barrier between dream and reality." However, Kyrou soon
checks himself: "To talk technique with reference to such
films would be stupid. This film *is*" (p. 232).

Everything Surrealists have to say about dreams under-
scores the double virtue of dreaming: "at the same time to cast
light on our inner reality and also to reveal new aspects of a
wider outer reality."[5] This is what so excites them in *Peter
Ibbetson*. With remarkable fidelity, the movie reflects their
views on the relationship of dreaming to living, and does so by
focusing on love. Only love, "that instant when sensual pleas-

The separated lovers: (top), Pierre, who has just heard of his mother's death is separated from Mimsey, in the garden, by a balustrade and window rail; (bottom), the adult Peter and Mary, still separated by a symbolic barrier.

ure consummates the union of dream and action," Rosey contends, can train our attention on the intermediary state where he locates human happiness.

Everyone would agree that in the cinema "there is no domain forbidden to our dreams."[6] The outstanding feature of *Peter Ibbetson*, however, is the following. Developing the theme of searching and finding, it uses a dream to mediate between desire and full acknowledgment of desire, so pointing to the demand for total fulfillment made by man's desires.

After the revelation of love, the couple plan to elope, regardless of cost to the security guaranteed them by society in the past. They are prepared to make whatever sacrifice love requires. Peter is ready to give up his profession as a successful architect. Mary is no less willing (denying her marriage vows) to forego the privilege of title. No histrionics, incidentally, accompany their decision: Gary Cooper's habitual acting style brings to the role of Peter a restraint that does as much to enhance the film version of one du Maurier novel as the grotesque performance by John Barrymore (who played Cooper's role in a screen version of *Peter Ibbetson* made in 1922 under the title *Forever*) in the title role of the movie *Svengali* (1931) does to detract from the film version of another, *Trilby*.

Given the period during which the action of *Peter Ibbetson* is set—some time before the turn of the century—the contravention of social taboos to which love commits Peter and Mary has the gravest consequences. Kyrou is hardly exaggerating when he characterizes their love as "a corrosive denial of accepted ideas, an admirable affirmation of real, mad love." His remark, in *Amour-Erotisme et cinéma*, reminds us of the last lines in an entry in the *Lexique succinct de l'érotisme* (1970): "eroticism, by its very individualism, escapes any appreciation (logical or moral) of a social character."[7] It brings to mind also some other definitions in the same lexicon, all of them pertinent to the Surrealists' interpretation of Hathaway's movie. Temptation is defined as "Inner solicitation that leads to accomplishment of a forbidden act, so that this interdict fans desire all the more."[8] Passion is called "State of absolute reaching out by one person to another who embodies all his reasons for living, and down to the most minute details, submits his conception of the universe to its authority" (p. 55). As for scandal, it is a "Sudden unveiling, for the purpose of provocation or defiance, of what society and conventional morality tolerate only camouflaged: the so-called shameful parts of the human body, the exploitation of man by man, the existence of torture, but also the too unbearable brilliance of a person out of tune with his environment."[9]

In Surrealism, temptation has nothing to do with sin. It is unreserved response to desire. To the Surrealist, Peter's conduct, and Mary's too, appears impeccable because neither of them holds back when love has identified its object. Passion now dominates their lives, admitting of no impediment. For this reason, the lovers find themselves out of tune with the environment where Peter's professional competence has earned him respect and status and Mary has occupied her assigned place as the wife of a man of rank. Their rejection of the benefits the world confers in return for conformism is scandalous because it sets them outside society. That is to say, their behavior is a scandal and, as such, subject to condemnation and punishment. When Peter accidentally kills Mary's husband (who had every intention of shooting them both, in righteous indignation at the young man's challenge to his proprietory rights), society's justice exacts payment in full. Peter is condemned to life imprisonment.

Up to the moment Peter and Mary avow their love for one another, the course of events in *Peter Ibbetson* respects the Surrealists' interpretation of love's outlaw status in Western civilization. Surrealists have no reason to object to anything Hathaway has shown so far. Yet his film presumably gives them no more cause for enthusiasm than the book on which it draws. In fact, chance—which, in reuniting Peter and Mary, seems to have worked no less beneficently than Surrealists are sure it must, in human affairs—appears to have ultimately disastrous consequences, separating the lovers and depriving Peter Ibbetson of his liberty. There seems to be good reason to wonder whether, in his and Mary's experience, love—mediating between desire and life—has not sprung a trap from which they cannot escape. It looks as though a dream has played its role in bringing a man and a woman together only long enough for them to be able to measure all that they have lost, now that society's laws have come between them. On the evidence presented during *Peter Ibbetson*'s second phase, it

All barriers removed.

is hard indeed to see why Benjamin Péret classes it with the early Chaplin films, with F. W. Murnau's *Nosferatu, eine Symphonie des Grauens* (1922) and with Luis Buñuel's *L'Age d'Or* as "an oasis in a desert of asphyxiating dust."[10]

It is only too clear that respect for the plot inherited from du Maurier imposes on Hathaway's movie a distinctly confining progression, up to the point where Peter Ibbetson is arrested and brought to trial. The action of the movie is set in a well-defined historical period during which societal relationships were rigidly controlled. Although this fact contributes to intensifying the drama that culminates in the sentence Peter has to face, fidelity to the novel does bring risks. Hathaway's film is committed to well-tried dramatic patterns, and a Surrealist inevitably must find these particularly suspect. The Surrealists' contempt for cinema conceived as filmed theater (a sad legacy, in their opinion, of the introduction of sound into movies) makes them especially sensitive to the melodramatic elements with which Hathaway had to work, when bringing *Peter Ibbetson* to the screen. At the same time, however, scorning convention, they are eagerly alert to any sign of radical departure from conventionality. They find such a sign in the shared dream that, thanks to du Maurier's innovative boldness, sets *Peter Ibbetson* on quite an unconventional path.

In short, Hathaway's movie has to advance to its third and final phase before it fully vindicates the claim made for it with such assurance in Breton's *L'Amour fou*. Then, from the moment when Peter is imprisoned, it lets us see why Kyrou cites it in *Amour-Erotisme et cinéma* as one of the very few films to have made him understand that cinema "can raise love to the highest summits" — love, he specifies, understood "in a universal concept, permanent and magnificently carnal" (p. 230).

It is no accident that a spokesman for Surrealism should emphasize the carnal aspect of love, as delineated in Hathaway's movie. Kyrou's aim is quite definite: to undermine Henri Agel's argument in a book titled *Le Cinéma a-t-il une âme?* that love in *Peter Ibbetson*, in John Cromwell's *The Enchanted Cottage* (1945), and in William Dieterle's *Portrait of Jenny* (1948) is spiritual, for this reason reflecting "a state of humility." True love, Kyrou counters, is "a victory over humility," dismissed in his book as "a hateful feeling" (p. 232). The love we find in *Peter Ibbetson*, he would have us believe, is true love. Thus, whereas the second phase of this movie seems to foreshadow the collapse of love — its defeat by forces society has mustered in its own defense — the last section of *Peter Ibbetson* celebrates love's triumph. This comes in a self-assertive act all the more insolent because it remains rationally inexplicable and so, to reason, indefensible. Moreover, love triumphs by turning to advantage the peculiar qualities possessed by cinema as a medium of narration.

Society having taken its revenge on Peter and coincidentally punished Mary just as cruelly, pessimistic conclusions seem to be inescapable. If any manifestation of humility in the lovers strikes a Surrealist as quite unacceptable, it appears all the same that nothing short of a miracle is likely to save them from the fate of helpless and hopeless submission. We witness a miracle, though, as, entering its third phase, *Peter Ibbetson* directs our attention almost exclusively to dreams.

The introduction of dreams and particular emphasis upon them are not sufficient in themselves to break down the limitations of melodrama. What really count in *Peter Ibbetson*, then, are the nature and function of the oneiric material and the way it is presented for the audience to see. Here, dreams serve to do two things at once. They explode the melodramatic frame within which the narrative has advanced up to now, showing it to have been no more than a convenient means of bringing a poignant love story into sharp focus. Then, in the third narrative phase, dreams create a mood that dispels the clouds of pessimism darkening the closing stages of the second phase. If it were not for all this, *Peter Ibbetson* would be very much less exciting to the Surrealists. Indeed, without its dreams we can be sure Hathaway's film would represent in their eyes, a betrayal of the conviction voiced in their name by Gui Rosey: "Desire, one can see, adds to our power over the world" (p. 94).

Before we consider how *Peter Ibbetson* sheds light on these words, it is helpful to examine, briefly, a movie of quite a different kind. Made in 1944 and set in contemporary society, Otto Preminger's *Laura* is a mystery story complete with murder, assorted suspects, and a detective, MacPherson, investigating a young woman's death. At one point in the film, MacPherson falls asleep in the woman's apartment, beneath her portrait. Quite against our expectations, Laura, in the person of Gene Tierney, opens the front door and enters.

The explanation proposed by Kyrou accords substantially with the one given by Gérard Legrand in an essay published in *L'Age du Cinéma* in 1951. Laura's unforeseen and quite unforeseeable arrival, Legrand remarks, stands for "the triumph of a lonely man's obsession," even though he does concede that what we take to be the detective's dream is "the only 'false' cinematic dream I know" (p. 100). Of course, when we find that Laura is not a projection of MacPherson's dream after all, we discover too that she is still alive. What is more, the film goes on to explain quite logically why she appears when and where she does. Kyrou, then, might appear guilty of falsifying Preminger's intentions while posing a rhetorical question in *Amour-Erotisme et cinéma*: "What does it matter if the story goes on to explain this *apparition*?" (p. 244). The interpretation of *Laura* in *Le Surréalisme au cinéma* ("the exaltation of total love, mad love" [p. 130]) is no more tendentious than the one in *Amour-Erotisme et cinéma*, where we are assured that Laura comes back "because a man, because all the men-spectators, in love with her, no longer could be satisfied with the memories of those who had known her" (p. 244). In order to condone such a view, one has to ignore a basic fact: in *Laura*, Preminger is wholeheartedly dedicated to establishing reasonable premises and proceeding to reasonable deductions. Kyrou's claims appear defensible only to those who favor and take pleasure in antirational explanations such as Preminger neither proposes nor, in the long run, authorizes in his movie.

And yet, before we speak of inexcusable distortion on a Surrealist's part, before we accuse Kyrou of falsifying the evidence offered or of ignoring, in Preminger's film, as much of that evidence as he chooses to reject, we have to look a little more closely at what happens in *Laura*.

We still have not been given any explanation for Laura's sudden appearance when something noteworthy occurs. In defiance of common sense, of the evidence available to us up to this point in the movie, the moment the apartment door opens, just like MacPherson's, our eyes testify to Laura's unaccountable presence. We do not understand at this stage why a woman we were led to believe dead has come home. All we know for sure is that we are unsure of what we know. However much good sense protests, Laura appears to have come back from the grave. Thus the cinema's power to materialize the detective's dream—that is, to satisfy his desire to see Laura for himself—produces a sequence contrasting sharply with other people's version of the past, making her appearance before us reasonably acceptable, within the cinematic convention of the flashback. What the eyes now show is inadmissible evidence, in reason's court. Rational thought tells us that the apparition MacPherson sees is impossible. And yet we ourselves see the same thing. And so, at the moment when sight challenges and defeats common sense, *Laura* demonstrates one of the special virtues of cinema as a mode of imaginatively stimulating communication.

Only later do we find ourselves asked to correct the impression our eyes have given. At this stage, we can appreciate where Kyrou and Legrand err, in looking upon Preminger's film as indulgently as they do. We discover that the movie's director has manipulated effect so as to persuade his audience to associate Laura's arrival with MacPherson's dreaming about her. Hence we cannot even speak confidently, now, of fruitful intervention by beneficent chance that gives Surrealists so much cause for optimism about life. Instead, we have to acknowledge that Otto Preminger has played a trick on his public, merely to infuse his film with greater suspense.

If then we wonder why, taken in by the joke, Kyrou stubbornly refuses to admit his gullibility, the answer is not hard to find. His eagerness to believe a supposedly dead woman has appeared just because a man, already attracted to her, dreams about her can point in one direction only. It testifies to the Surrealists' abiding belief in desire.

Oddly enough, the word "dream" does not figure in the *Lexique succinct de l'érotisme*. However, the word "desire" does come under consideration. R. Schwaller de Lubicz is quoted as saying that desire is "a string stretched between two complements and the sound of this string is life." Hence all it takes to produce the sound is to "make it vibrate with some shock and this shock is the Erotic" (p. 67). In the same context, Legrand refers to desire as alone defining the individual human being. He calls it "ceaselessly a ruin and ceaselessly a phoenix" (p. 21).

Returning now to *Peter Ibbetson*, to look more closely at the significance of desire and related concepts in Surrealist thought, we come to a fuller understanding of the value Surrealists attach to dreaming and of the capital role of dreams in this movie.

A few more extracts from the *Lexique succinct de l'érotisme* help place *Peter Ibbetson* in the perspective from which Surrealists look at it. As might be expected, the first refers to imagination, defined as follows by Gérard Legrand: "Power particularly dreaded by preachers, economists, and, in a general way, all who want to impede the free functioning of thought or sexual sense. The apparitions it arouses are in fact outside our control, but often have the strength to control us without any argument" (p. 35). Such a definition suggests that, after his conviction, Peter and Mary can hope to defeat society through reliance upon imagination to realize their desires. Through imagination, they can enter a rapturous state, in which ecstasy takes on the meaning Legrand gives it: "('To be outside oneself'). Immobility wavering between total lucidity and its opposite, in which the horizons of time and place fade away. It is agreed that this can be seen as the highest state erotic man can attain" (pp. 27-28). This definition will be particularly relevant to the situation of the lovers in Hathaway's film, once Peter has been paralyzed by a beating at the hands of his guards who leave him confined to his cell, for the rest of his life immobilized on his back.

At first, Peter's enforced, inescapable immobility seems only to aggravate the desperate conditions he has to tolerate in prison, with no hope of pardon. In addition, it appears to emphasize his isolation, his distance from Mary. Under these circumstances, the idea of contact between the two seems quite unthinkable and the following definition of embrace by José Pierre looks superfluous: "Action of pressing firmly between one's arms. By extension designates the complete amorous exchange between two lovers." However, Pierre makes it clear that he sees "embrace" as stressing "the unconscious desire to reduce space, an obstacle between the lovers, so as to form henceforth only one person and one place" (p. 27).

In fact, then, the lovers of *Peter Ibbetson* do know the joys and satisfaction of embracing. They come to know ecstasy in the full sense that Legrand gives the word, reaping all its rewards. They do this without ever having the physical contact assumed necessary for erotic fulfillment. Overthrowing all the obstacles society has placed between them, they see time and space abolished, and they become one, in one place—in their dreams.

The last phase of *Peter Ibbetson* repudiates the pessimistic conclusions to which the second phase pointed. Instead of depicting the frustration of love, the film is bathed, now, in a radiant optimism so perfectly in accord with Surrealist beliefs that it could not have been more faithful to Surrealist edicts if it had been made by Ado Kyrou, director of several films of Surrealist inspiration. During its third phase, this film shows Peter and Mary meeting one another in their dreams, able to do so at will and at any time of day or night. At this stage, *Peter Ibbetson* does more than simply expand beyond the confining boundaries of melodramatic theater. It also pushes farther than the bounds of credibility allow. Kyrou, naturally, exults in the fact. Noting in *Amour-Erotisme et cinéma* that the dreams shared by Peter and Mary are "a challenge to rationalism, to positivism," he declares in the same breath that they are, for this very reason, "a glorification of reality" (p. 232).

The problem with this interpretation of Hathaway's film is that few readers are willing or even able to take, without hesitation, a step for which Kyrou, as a Surrealist, assumes us all to be ready. In order to do so, they would have to accept Surrealist theory without demur, agreeing that glorification of reality entails rejection of rationalism and denial of positivism. Fortunately, it is not a matter of having to make a choice, once and for all, between Agel's contention that love in *Peter Ibbetson* serves to introduce us to the spiritual and Kyrou's contrary inference that it leads, instead, to the Surreal (which he defines as "the concrete aspects of a reality conceived in its totality, embracing dream, imagination, aspirations . . ."). If Agel's argument seems lacking in weight, this does not mean the only alternative must be entertaining the notion that *Peter Ibbetson* necessarily illustrates Kyrou's thesis. Taking sides is not the issue. What counts, rather, is establishing Kyrou's reasons for claiming that the Surreal manifests itself during the closing stages of *Peter Ibbetson*.

Two sentences from Breton's *"Comme dans un bois"* help us along our way. The first emphasizes that Surrealists react on the basis of faith to the evidence brought before them by film. "There is a way of going to the movies as others go to church and I think that, from a certain angle, quite independently of what is playing, it is there that the only *absolutely modern* mystery is celebrated." The second sentence follows immediately. "There is no doubt that desire and love cover one's outlay in this mystery."

If, now, instead of wondering whether we should go as far as Kyrou in responding to *Peter Ibbetson*, we wonder how he comes to look the way he does upon Hathaway's version of du Maurier's novel, we find ourselves facing a familiar question once again. We have to ask more insistently than before about the appeal cinema holds for Surrealists, when compared with other modes of narrative communication. Our best starting point, now, is a page from *"Comme dans un bois."* Here Breton talks of *"going beyond* the stage of the 'permitted' that, nowhere else as in the cinema, seems to me to tempt us to the 'forbidden'."

The means peculiar to film make it possible for cinema to

"*go beyond*" by presenting its audience with the spectacle of the "forbidden," eliminating whatever separates us from its manifestation in our day-to-day lives. In *Peter Ibbetson*, the results not only remove the obstacle of space we would expect to see keeping the lovers apart, but also lends support to an idea advanced in Kyrou's *Amour-Erotisme et cinéma*: "An instant of mad love is eternity" (p. 232). Thus, watching the closing sequences of Hathaway's movie, we grasp the reason why *Peter Ibbetson* impresses Surrealists more as a film than it ever could do as a novel. As cinema, *Peter Ibbetson* demonstrates film's unique capacity to present, visually, evidence of a kind that a written text could not show us and so would have to rely on our imagination to supply. Without ever having to affirm this in any way, it lets us *see* that, meeting in their dreams over a period of years, Peter and Mary stay as young as when they first recognized one another.

There is a vast difference between a novel that assures us, however earnestly, that love keeps those it sustains ageless in a private world of dreams and a movie that *shows* them to be impervious to passing time. Asserting that Peter and Mary are untouched by physical decline leads the writer into the realm of the rationally forbidden. Here he is at a disadvantage because he can succeed only if, in his reader's mind, reason then can be persuaded to suspend all rights, granting imagination the widest possible latitude.

Cinema, of course, does not rule out imaginative participation by its audience—far from it. Film is fully capable, too, of supplementing imagination no less than of stimulating its activity. Indeed, the supreme advantage possessed by film over all other media lies in its ability to show as it tells. To the extent that seeing is believing, the film experience impresses itself upon us with irresistible immediacy. In this sense, it short-circuits rational objections, when it does not bypass them altogether. During movie projection, the eye registers even things that reason will not condone. For the eye is unencumbered by the burden of rationalism. As Breton makes a point of stressing in the very first sentence of his study of Surrealism's relations with painting, *Le Surréalisme et la peinture* (1928), "The eye exists in an untamed state."

Henry Levin's film *The Guilt of Janet Ames* (1947) was distributed in France under the title *Peter Ibbetson avait raison* [Peter Ibbetson was right]. Whatever that title could mean to anyone in the audience who had not had the opportunity to see *Peter Ibbetson*, one thing is beyond dispute. It paid tribute to Hathaway's movie as a film deserving to be remembered longer than Preminger's *Laura*.

It is interesting to observe that, despite their admiration for *Laura*, both Kyrou and Legrand are mistaken about the substance of the radio broadcast made at the end of the film by the murderer, Waldo Lydecker. Each states that Lydecker underlines the brevity of love. While it is true that he closes with some verses from Dowson depicting life as transitory in all its aspects, Lydecker prefaces his quotation with these words: "And so, as history has proved, love is eternal. It has been the strongest motivation for human actions through centuries. Love is stronger than life. It reaches beyond the dark shadow of death."

As Laura listens to the broadcast, Lydecker is letting himself into her apartment to make a second attempt on the life of a woman he is willing to share with no one. Obviously, Surrealists must reserve approval for this man's ideas, while reproving the course of action to which they incite him. But this is not the main reason why Preminger's film must rank below Hathaway's, in the Surrealists' estimation. The time comes when Peter Ibbetson searches his dream in vain for Mary, who has died. He hears her voice calling him, understands, and quietly dies also. Thus Hathaway's movie far surpasses Preminger's in applying cinematographic technique to the benefit of Surrealist thought. Whereas *Laura* resorts to the spoken word to convey the message that love is eternal, *Peter Ibbetson* lets us see love triumph over "the last enemy that shall be destroyed." While Preminger states his conclusion, Hathaway demonstrates *his*. *Laura* closes as literature, with the verbal formulation of an argument that the final shot of a broken clock only reinforces. *Peter Ibbetson* remains to the very end a film that uses cinematic means to bring to our attention a message in which no Surrealist can fail to recognize the triumph of Surrealist thought.

5

Delmer Daves: *Dark Passage* (1947)

NO ONE could be accused of blind antagonism to Surrealism for observing that *King Kong, Duck Soup,* and *Peter Ibbetson* all stand at some distance from the reality that the vast majority of us know. Everybody, of course, grants willingly enough that motion pictures generally concentrate on periods of unusual tension or excitement and, in so doing, distort our humdrum existence to some degree, most often showing individuals caught up in events very few of us indeed have experienced personally. Even allowing for this, though, it is fair to say that the three films mentioned do more than simply accelerate the normal pace of pedestrian living. Whatever the accent with which they speak to a Surrealist, it is nevertheless perfectly appropriate to call them products of the Hollywood dream factory. Freedonia is no less distant than Skull Island from the world where we find ourselves perpetually shut in by rules, restrictions, and obligations through which society imposes its imperious demands.

Many people are going to draw the same conclusion from this evidence. They will infer that, if a Surrealist can find nothing of interest in movies reflecting their own experience more accurately, then he must be attracted, really, to fairytales of one kind or another and not to those "tales to be written for grown-ups," demanded by André Breton in his *Manifeste du surréalisme* of 1924.[1] We can expect to hear, as we have heard before, vaguely formulated but energetically defended complaints tending to dismiss Surrealism as no more than a sophisticated form of evasion. One must be prepared to hear, this time, accusations serving to back up the argument that a Surrealist takes refuge in a movie house with the express purpose of seeking escape from the hostile world around him, to with-

101

Showing Vincent Parry with a revolver that he does not carry in the film, this publicity photo invokes Humphrey Bogart's legend in the movies, despite the fact that in Dark Passage, *he plays a man whom love turns away from anticipated action.* Credit: Movie Star News

draw for a while into a fairyland that offers the prospect of temporary release from the burden of daily living.

There is an important difference, however, between fairytales meant for children (and appealing to adults who are no more demanding of film fare than their children) and the "almost fairytales" for grown-ups of which the first Surrealist manifesto speaks. In fact, the critical element here is the distinction, however small and unimportant it may seem at first, to which the word "almost" draws attention.

When the Surrealists' ambitions and accomplishments come under consideration, no greater error could be made than that of believing these men and women determined at all cost to turn their backs once and for all on the real world we face every day. Above all else, Surrealism confronts us with the question of what is real. "In its primary sense," one of its spokesmen explains, "surrealism is a realism that refuses to abide by 'summary realities', that knows, explores or plans to explore countries of the real whose interest or existence vulgar realism contests."[2] In the works its practitioners place before us, Surrealism imposes a sufficiently new angle on external reality to persuade unprejudiced observers to acknowledge the following. Reality need not impress itself upon the human sensibility as hopelessly confined to the contingent and as irremediably oppressive in its effect.

In other words, Surrealists become especially attentive and respond to certain commercial films from the moment when these introduce into daily life a liberative factor pointing in the direction of fairytale freedom from the restraints of "summary reality." Such movies take on particular value for the Surrealist because they nevertheless do not sever all links with the everyday world. The source of their appeal lies just where Breton's words lead us to expect to find it. Yet as the action takes shape and direction, gathering momentum, the story solicits interest by tugging at the spectator's imagination, stimulating its activity beyond limits to which his original impression of being on familiar ground seemed to condemn him.

The distinction between liberation and escapism is now easier to discern. It can be recognized as one of the perennial sources of Surrealist optimism. Escapism comes from seeking and enjoying the fruits of temporary evasion—a respite, perhaps, but without any long term benefits. On the other hand, a liberation nourishing imaginative freedom promises more substantial gains. The latter are of a less ephemeral nature, because they open doors we now discover need never again be closed tight. They invite speculation of a kind that makes greater and greater demands on life, while supporting the belief that such demands *can* be met. And they remind us of a declaration by André Breton in his *Second Manifeste du surréalisme*, written in 1929: "I believe in the absolute virtue of everything practiced, spontaneously or not, in the direction of nonacceptance" (p. 156).

The fundamental difference lies here. Whereas evasion condemns us to return, in the end, to face problems we should like to avoid, liberation marks an advance, progress toward the solution of a problem, even if not its total elimination. According to Breton's *Arcane 17*, first published in New York in 1944, the idea of liberty is "an idea fully master of itself, that reflects an unconditional view of what *qualifies* man and alone lends meaning to human *development*. Liberty is not like liberation, a struggle with illness, it is health."[3]

When one studies remarks Surrealists have uttered about Hollywood movies it seems increasingly difficult to make sense of their reactions. Of course, we find it relatively easy to anticipate many of their objections and to forecast with some degree of confidence that they will reject this or that movie for quite predictable reasons. But our understanding of Surrealism advances little, really, with the discovery that those who subscribe to its principles are unimpressed by a film about Joan of Arc, whether made by Dreyer or by Rossellini. Indeed, far from helping clarify our ideas about their taste in cinema, the eagerness with which Surrealists voice approval of a singularly varied selection of movies actually can be confusing. This is especially the case when we take account of their enthusiasm for isolated sequences in films which, otherwise, interest them not at all.

However, seen from the angle Breton invites us to adopt, the diversity of films that Surrealists salute as meritorious no longer puzzles or tempts us to infer that they respond erratically, in the absence of an identifiable behavior pattern to whatever the cinema brings before them. The diversity we face, now, appears less bewildering as soon as one central fact is acknowledged. In this instance, diversity is not merely the

reflection of the rich variety of Hollywood's movie produc-
tivity. Far more significantly, it mirrors the complexity of the
problems confronting any Surrealist, the moment he attempts
to assert a freedom that everything about him seems to con-
spire to obstruct.

Basically, Surrealist response is the outgrowth of desire.
Any film, therefore, in which a Surrealist can detect an echo of
his own aspirations earns his sympathetic attention, provided
the conclusion it proposes, implies or suggests does not denote unacceptable compromise with society's restrictive demands, after the fashion of *Stazione termini*. Like *Brief Encounter*, this movie is, to Surrealists, an unconscionable act of
capitulation such as they praise Stuart Heisler (who edited
Peter Ibbetson) for sparing us at the end of *I Died a Thousand
Times* (1955), his version of Raoul Walsh's *High Sierra* (1941).
With characteristically unrestrained enthusiasm, in *Le Surréalisme au cinéma* (1963), Ado Kyrou salutes Heisler's movie
as "the finest postwar 'gangster film' " (p. 60), telling us that it
deals with someone who "sublime in his solitude, romantic
contrary to the custom of this century," discovers "a love that
does not betray him" but permits him to "die like a man,
rather than live in chains" (p. 131).

At issue here is something quite different from the crude
distinction between law-abiding citizens to whom (however
difficult the situation) certain solutions are unthinkable and
the outlaw figure who, having set himself against society, enjoys total freedom of action. What matters is the difference
separating, on one side, the individual who assumes full responsibility for his own fate and, on the other, people who
conduct themselves like the couples in De Sica's film and
Lean's. Valuing self-preservation over self-fulfillment, the latter are open to all the insidious temptations by which society
schools us in conformist conduct. Their energy is sapped and
they fall back on the supposedly sterling virtues of caution and
acceptance. In so doing, they commit a cardinal sin that Surrealists consider quite unpardonable: their actions mark a betrayal of love. In his second Surrealist manifesto, Breton confided that he looked upon renouncing love, whether or not on
the authority of an ideological pretext, as "one of the rare in-
expiable crimes a man endowed with some intelligence can
commit in the course of his lifetime" (p. 213).

Results of an "Inquiry," a survey of capital importance to the Surrealists, were published in the twelfth and last issue of *La Révolution surréaliste* (December 15, 1929), where they appeared next to Breton's second manifesto. The survey placed on record responses to a questionnaire asking, "What sort of hope do you place in love?" and related questions. It made public the fact that, in Surrealism, love is the touchstone of human conduct. In the same number of the first French Surrealist magazine appeared the scenario of *Un Chien andalou* whose coauthor, Luis Buñuel, answered one of the inquiry's question with the declaration, "I would gladly sacrifice my liberty to love. I have already done so."

Love that serves to measure an individual's stature is not, for Surrealists, mere sentimental attachment. In an unsigned note prefacing the findings of the 1929 inquiry, Breton spoke of the idea of love as "the only one capable of reconciling any man, momentarily or not, to the idea of life." He stressed that Surrealists restore to love its "strict and menacing meaning of total attachment to a human being 'in a soul and in a body', the soul and body of that person." Similarly, in his *Anthologie de l'Amour sublime* (1956), Benjamin Péret celebrated "the double aspect of sublime love, at once carnal and spiritual" (p. 16), emphasizing that the value of sublime love is located "at an ultimate point where mind and heart come together and are allied" (p. 62).

The reason why the carnal aspects of love are given prominence in Surrealism is easy to perceive. Surrealists take care to oppose the teachings of the church, which link love, through woman, with original sin. Péret asserts in his *Anthologie*, "Christianity thus becomes a religion of repression like no other" (p. 34). In contrast, love manifests itself to the Surrealist as a revelation compelling those it touches to reconsider their place and role in society, where religion operates as a powerful conservative force. Referring to the sudden revelation of love at first sight, Péret argues that, from the moment a man experiences it, he "can no longer find his former self again," having been "the object of a sudden metamorphosis." Meanwhile a similar transformation takes place in the woman he loves and who loves him (pp. 72-73). Theirs is what Breton calls in *L'Amour fou* "convulsive love," that is to say, love guaranteed by something he terms "circumstantial magic" and defines as circumstances entering into magical relationships with one another, under the influence of desire. And so, a man and a woman who have fallen in love necessarily find themselves reviewing their societal relationships and the role *vis-à-vis* the rest of the world that they have played in the past.

The contrast proves to be instructive if, after *Brief Encounter*, we watch a film Surrealists consider an admirable and quite exceptional achievement by a director whose work they do not respect as they do Vigo's or Tod Browning's or James Whale's. The director is Delmer Daves and his film *Dark Passage* (1947).

Dark Passage tells of a man, Vincent Parry, who escapes from San Quentin after serving three years of a life sentence for murdering his wife. Its plot is advanced by two most convenient coincidences. While on the run, Parry has the good fortune to meet a young woman called Irene Jansen, whose father died in prison after being convicted of murdering her stepmother. Irene is no less convinced of Parry's innocence than of her father's. Soon we learn that she is a friend of Madge Rapf, whose evidence at Parry's trial brought his conviction.

Interestingly, Daves, who himself wrote the screenplay, offers no explanation for the second of these coincidences, correctly estimating that his audience would tolerate it because of the benefits it brings to plot development in *Dark Passage*. The first coincidence, however, leads Irene to make a statement which, instead of helping divert our attention from it, stresses its inexplicable consequence—further coincidence. This woman whom Parry has never seen before appears suddenly before him, calls him by his first name, and declares, "Look, I'm trying to give you a chance." Parry's reply ("Well, I don't get it, but—let's go") shows him willing to place himself unreservedly in her hands. Later, in the safety of Irene's apartment, Parry will learn that the morning of his escape, she had awakened wondering how he was getting along and then had decided to go painting in the very area where they finally met. After claiming she does not believe in fate or destiny, "or any of those things," Irene confesses, "I guess it was something like fate. Maybe it was something because I was thinking of you. I don't know." As she speaks, we hear for the first time, quietly in the background, the phonograph playing *You're So Marvelous*.

Realizing how unfair it is to compromise Irene, Parry leaves her apartment, not at all sure where to head, and hails a taxi. Recognizing him, the driver offers to arrange for him to undergo plastic surgery. While Sam is completing arrangements, Parry calls on his closest friend, George Fellsinger, who agrees to let him use his flat for a week while recovering from the operation. Returning from the doctor's office to find Fellsinger dead, Parry has no alternative but to seek refuge at Irene's once again.

When his bandages have been removed, Parry asks to hear *You're So Marvelous* once more ("I may not hear it again for a long time"). As the record plays, the following dialogue takes place:

IRENE: "I *thought* I had a good life here, but your going away doesn't make it seem good any more. I — sort of joined your team and — I don't look forward to being without you."

PARRY: "When I leave here you're *off* my team and *lucky* to be. You know, I've got the Indian sign on me. It seems I can't win. I've got to start out and prove who killed them."

Parry seems willing, now, to accept and follow Irene's advice ("Don't even try, Vincent"). He says the best thing for him to do is "get the first bus out of town, fast!" At first evasive about his destination, he admits, when challenged, "All right, I do know." Is he suspicious of Irene, who might reveal where he has gone? She cannot accept this: "No, it isn't. You won't tell me because you think I'll come there. You think I'll follow you." Parry exclaims, "You'd be insane to follow me!" Irene responds: "And insane to pick you up on the road? Was I crazy to let you stay here?" Parry nods and they exchange their first kiss before he concedes, "Yes."

Still not having told Irene where he is going, Parry checks in to a cheap hotel. There he is approached by Baker, a petty crook who has been following him since his escape from prison. Baker intends to blackmail Irene. During a struggle, Baker is accidentally killed, but not before telling Parry of a car he saw outside the building where Fellsinger lived. The car belongs to Madge Rapf. Going to the woman's home, Parry forces her to confess to killing both his wife and Fellsinger. However, Madge accidentally falls out of a window. Her death leaving him with no chance of clearing his name, Vincent

Parry heads for the bus station. There he inserts a coin in the jukebox, which plays *You're So Marvelous* while he phones Irene: "I'm just beginning to realize it's better to have something to look forward to." He tells her to look up on the map a little coastal town in Peru, where he will be waiting for her: "There's a little café, right on the bay."

From the first, the commercialism of Daves's movie is quite apparent. No effort is made to conceal the fact that *Dark Passage* is a vehicle designed to display the talents of two film stars, one of whom enjoys an unquestionably established reputation. Their presence is a guarantee of wide appeal and box office returns. Moreover, the acting style of the male lead is sufficiently familiar to movie audiences to give the film its tonality. The latter affects the plot as much as it does the actors' interpretation, since, no less than his natural gifts, the public's expectations impose definite limits on Humphrey Bogart's roles.

As it turns out, Bogart's participation is not a disadvantage at all, where the Surrealist dimension of *Dark Passage* is concerned. In this movie his acting is restrained, muted even. Hence his performance contributes directly to making one important thing plain. To appeal to Surrealists, a film does not have to be baroque, sensational, or strikingly unusual either in substance or in treatment. Introducing Jean Ferry's story collection *Le Mécanicien et autres contes* (1950—Ferry is none other than the Jean Lévy whom *King Kong* so impressed), André Breton voiced his respect for "works electrified by the need for subversion" which he saw as capable of "showing the capacity of individual resistance opposed to general domestication." *Dark Passage* demonstrates that elements consonant with Surrealist subversion can be present in a run-of-the-mill Hollywood movie that, to the inattentive eye, seems pedestrian in both content and presentation.

Described by a follower of André Breton—Gérard Legrand, writing in the special Surrealism issue of *L'Age du Cinéma* (1951)—as "a multilevel masterpiece," *Dark Passage* incorporates two themes of particular interest to Surrealists. It tells of an escaped convict who, to evade recapture, undergoes plastic surgery that gives him new facial features and who falls in love with a woman who does not have to be persuaded of his innocence. To the Surrealist, this means that Daves's film treats of man's search for identity, associated with the reasons why he has to come to terms with a new face (cutting away the bandages, Irene comments, "It's a pretty big moment for you, starting a new life with a new face"), and with an emergent sense of selfhood, nurtured by a woman's loving devotion: it is Irene who suggests to Parry "a new name to go with your new face."

Such a view of *Dark Passage* is visibly tendentious. Of course, few who have seen the film are going to protest that the Surrealists flagrantly distort the intentions underlying the screenplay. All the same, it might be argued that, following the Surrealists' lead, we have to be prepared to see the center of gravity shift in this movie, so that its major theme—the injustice suffered by its hero and the steps he takes to vindicate himself, while falling in love—appears out of true. Be that as it may, a Surrealist's reading of *Dark Passage* is enlightening. Illuminating the film's puzzling ending, it invests this movie with a positive subversive quality to which no one is more sensitive than he.

To appreciate why Surrealists are disposed to view *Dark Passage* the way they do, we must begin by understanding the following. One of the fundamental impulses behind their much publicized detestation of the church is lost from sight if we do not give full value to their admiration for Benjamin Christiansen's movie *Haxan*, made in Denmark as early as 1923, for the Frenchman Claude Autant-Lara's *L'Auberge rouge* (1952), and even for the Swede Goesta Bernard's *Lattjiomed Boccaccio* (1950), which shows monks dancing the samba. Surrealists are persuaded that each individual must control his own destiny. They are convinced we gain nothing by looking to any institution to extend guarantees or even the possibility of salvation—whatever weight one is inclined to give that word. Furthermore, man's need to find salvation through self-fulfillment and self-liberation must be met here and now. For the hope of any adjustment in status, upon transfer to a life beyond the grave, is meaningless to the Surrealist mind. In *Amour-Erotisme et cinéma* (1966) Ado Kyrou restates a familiar Surrealist axiom when he asserts that love is "the first adversary of religion" (p. 110).

André Breton is much concerned in *Arcane 17* with "that

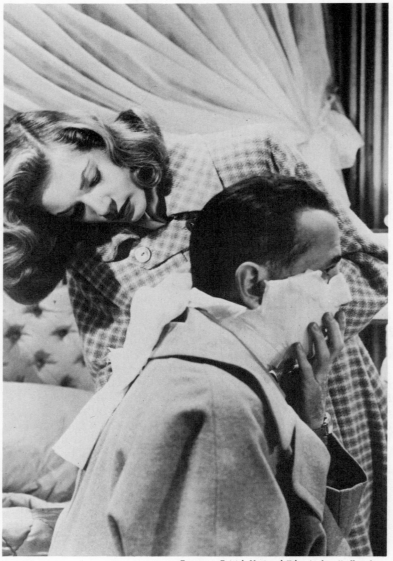

"It's a pretty big moment for you. . . ."

which tends to make the flesh sacred to the same degree as the soul, to have them considered indissociable." Hence this book shows Breton preoccupied with "the idea of *salvation on earth* by woman, the idea of the transcendent vocation of wo-man" (p. 70). Another important Breton book, *Nadja* (1928), details his disturbing relationship with a strange young woman who later had to be confined to a mental home. It be-gins with a fruitfully ambiguous question, *"Qui suis-je?"* which asks not only who I am but whom I am following. The sense of Breton's undertaking is clear, then. He means to show that identity is not given but is conquered, and only by those who search. To search, in other words, is a responsibility, just as self-identification is its anticipated reward. In Surrealism, the poet according to one of its leading practitioners, Benja-min Péret, "fights for man to attain a forever perfectible knowledge of himself and of the universe."[4]

People who erroneously take *Nadja* for a novel fail to recog-nize the anticipative character of Breton's text, written from the same typically Surrealist perspective that highlights the theme of self-discovery in *Dark Passage*. In Daves's film, the subjective camera brings narrative exposition into focus dur-ing the opening phase of the movie's action. The camera is used to record what the eyes of the escaped convict sees, while at the same time concealing his face from the theater audience. Of course, camera trickery stimulates the latter's curiosity and obviously is meant to do so. To the Surrealist, though, its valuable contribution lies elsewhere. It identifies our viewpoint with Parry's, before we are aware who he is and even before we have a clear idea of his situation.

It is no less significant that Daves abandons manipulative camera technique before long. After the operation that has re-molded Parry's face, making it unrecognizable to those who knew him before, a radical change of focus is introduced. We no longer see the world with his eyes but, quite convention-ally, from an angle that allows us to observe him from outside, his head bandaged now, after the style of the hero's in certain scenes from Whale's *The Invisible Man* (1933).

The audience may have shared the patient's apprehension about the outcome of the operation, his nightmarish dream under anaesthesia having raised the fear that, wielded by a demented hand, the scalpel will have transformed him into a freak. Removal of the bandages brings reassurance, after all: he looks just like Bogey. It brings something more, too. For while we can see, now, what face Parry has and recognize its familiar characteristics, Parry himself does not detect the resemblance. True, had he done so, he immediately would have set *Dark Passage* on a farcical course quite divergent from that prescribed by the David Goodis novel from which the movie was adapted. But this is not the crucial point. The fact that Parry's new face is familiar to us (as his voice has been, from the start), while yet strange to him, separates the film character impersonated by Bogart from the audience watching what happens to him. In one sense, we "know" who Parry is, just as we "know" that Irene Jansen is Lauren Bacall. Parry, though, still has to adjust to having a face that looks quite unfamiliar in the mirror, one he must learn to accept as his own.

There is nothing uniquely Surrealist by any means in being fascinated by the prospect of a new start in life, the slate wiped clean. In *Dark Passage*, what matters to the Surrealist spectator is this. The possibility of a new beginning comes to Parry at the very time he makes the discovery of love. Through love, freed of the past, he finds himself experiencing rebirth at all levels of the personality. Watching him, we are reminded that Breton's poem *Fata Morgana* (written in 1940 and banned by the Vichy Government censor) speaks of love as "that promise which goes beyond our comprehension." Later, in *Arcane 17* Breton shares with readers his conviction that love is "the true panacea," going on to affirm, "All fallacious, unbearable ideas of redemption aside, it is precisely through love and through love alone that is realized in the highest degree the fusion of existence and essence, ... I am speaking naturally of love that assumes all power . . ." (p. 38). Although it stigmatizes him from society's standpoint, in *Dark Passage* Vincent Parry's outlaw status works to his advantage. He no longer has to make certain choices, consciously or otherwise. Certain commitments no longer need review, and he does not have to meet certain of the obligations society routinely exacts. His face remolded, he is free to make his life over again.

Not everyone will see this as an opportunity to benefit from a second chance—a chance for Parry to take his place once again in society and to become a useful citizen. Even so, every one of us can find something to envy in a situation that holds out the possibility of correcting the past and making up for it.

This, however, is the stage at which to heed the warning set forth in *Arcane 17*, written at a time when the liberation of France from German occupation seemed imminent: "Take care, liberty for a prisoner is an admirably concrete thing, something positive so long as he is behind bars, but in the full light of day outside, the joys he expected of it wear out easily!" (p. 166). It was not Breton's intention to preach doleful pessimism about the future in a profoundly optimistic book, written just after he had met the woman to whom he would remain married for the last twenty years and more of his life. He was simply reaffirming something Surrealism had taught from the beginning. He wished to point out the necessity for vigilance, the need to be on the alert to temptations that may ensnare us at the very moment when we think we run no risk of being trapped.

There is more than a little exaggeration in Gérard Legrand's assertion that *Dark Passage* remains "accessible" only up to the moment of Madge Rapf's accidental death. Even so, his motive is not hard to track down. He wishes to suggest that the closing section of the film is disconcerting because "it can be justified only from the Surrealist point of view." While this interpretation is contentious, it does bid us consider how the Surrealist viewpoint justifies Parry's conduct, once he seems to have been deprived of the opportunity to exonerate himself.

It is evidently permissible to evaluate Vincent Parry's behavior, after he makes Irene Jansen's acquaintance, in light of certain pronouncements that Surrealists have made when presenting love as a force capable of guiding human beings compellingly and beneficently. Still, we have heard representative Surrealists say very little, really, that assures their attitude to love sufficient originality to convince an objective witness that similar remarks, equally fervent, could not have come from individuals owing no allegiance at all to Surrealism. Something else, too, must be apparent to any healthily skeptical observer. If there is indeed a parallel to be drawn, here, it must be regarded as purely accidental; it is not evidenced persuasively in what we see Parry *do*, once he has fallen in love with Irene. On the contrary, the motive for his conduct—the desire to clear his name—is one that seems no more natural

Credit: Museum of Modern Art/Film Stills Archive

Confrontations: (top), Irene Jansen faces a new Vincent Perry; (bottom), Perry and shrewish Marge Rapf.

because he happens to be in love than it would be if he were an incorrigible misogynist.

Parry's efforts to clear his name seem so normal that we attach no special significance to his behavior until provoked into giving it closer attention when, against our expectations, he abandons the struggle for reacceptance by the society that wrongfully found him guilty. If we review, now, a few more declarations to which love has inspired Breton and Péret, we discover something important. Beneath the surface drama enacted in *Dark Passage* for the entertainment of a wide audience, Surrealists detect a struggle that, to them, far outweighs in significance the incidents so carefully plotted in the screenplay.

First, though, we must notice the elliptical style of the final section of *Dark Passage*. It contrasts with the expository narrative mode utilized up to the moment when Parry phones Irene to invite her to join him in exile. From that moment onward, Daves practices rigorous compression. Parry is shown on a bus taking him to Benton, Arizona, where we know he plans to obtain forged identification papers before crossing into Mexico. Then we see him sitting at a table in a Latin American ambience, moodily sipping a drink. Abruptly, the band breaks off the music it has been playing and takes up *You're So Marvelous*. We read puzzlement on Parry's face, then recognition. He looks up and sees Irene standing at the other side of the room. As she walks toward him, he rises. Without a word, they dance. After the final fadeout, we continue to hear, "You're so marvelous, / Too marvelous for words."

Daves's direction does not impose on *Dark Passage* notably fast pacing, which might have endangered coherent exposition of a relatively complex plot. The contrast is therefore all the more striking, when he comes to his film's last two scenes, omitting several potentially dramatic sequences (Parry obtaining illegal papers, crossing the border, proceeding from Mexico to Paita, Peru, and prospering there enough to be able to buy the well-cut clothes he is wearing when we see him again). Is Daves guilty of hurrying, and therefore of failing to face questions his audience legitimately may ask? He has not told us why Parry makes for a small town in a country which, having lived all his life in San Francisco, he has never visited. Nor have we been prepared to believe Parry knows Spanish well enough to survive, let alone be a success (at what?) in Latin America.

A Surrealist is not perturbed by such apparent indications of haste. Nor is his pleasure reduced in any way by Daves's failure to forestall certain objections. On the contrary, for him unanswered questions enrich this film at the end, as they did at the beginning: What made Irene Jansen drive along the road by which Vincent Parry had escaped from San Quentin? What prompted her to back up her car, after passing an abandoned automobile, so as to appear miraculously before Parry just in time to prevent him from striking its unconscious driver with a rock?

Once love has entered Parry's life, the mysteries that Daves neglects to elucidate become part of his existence. Love, Surrealists would contend, transforms his life by infusing it with poetry, equated in Péret's *Anthologie des Mythes, légendes et contes populaires d'Amérique* (1960) with "an outlaw existence."

According to Péret, the "heart and nervous system of all poetry" is the marvelous.[5] And what is the marvelous? In the words of another Surrealist, Louis Aragon, it is "born of the refusal of *one* reality, but also of the development of a new relationship, of a new reality that this refusal has liberated."[6] Péret, for his part, declines to attempt a definition, yet remarks in his *Anthologie des Mythes,* "However, the marvelous is everywhere, hidden from the eyes of the vulgar, but ready to explode like a time bomb" (p. 15). The marvelous can be seen as life itself, he argues, on condition that it does not render life deliberately sordid, "as society strains its ingenuity to do with its schools, religions, law-courts, wars, occupations and liberations, concentration camps, and horrible and material intellectual wretchedness" (p. 16). It enters Vincent Parry's experience with the physical appearance of Irene Jansen. And how does it come to dominate his life? *Dark Passage* makes the answer eminently clear. Borne by the movie's theme song, the marvelous sweeps away, for Surrealists, all reservations, objections, and questions that soon come to appear impertinent.

The surprise we feel upon learning that, having given up the struggle, Parry intends to turn his back on life in the United States to become a fugitive in South America brings to light a prejudice society has managed to inculcate in most people. They assume society to be within its rights in making upon each individual demands it is both natural and proper for him to try to meet. In so doing, every Surrealist believes, they subscribe or tacitly submit to conservative moral values dubbed "repugnant" by Benjamin Péret, who states in his *Anthologie des Mythes, légendes et contes populaires d'Amérique*, "Only the assistance of an immense mechanism of material and intellectual coercion (the clergy and the schools supporting the police and the law-courts) has allowed them to stand until our time" (p. 25). Here, though, love takes on an active role, in protest against all forms of coercion. "Sublime love." argues Péret, "must then engage in a totally unequal fight with the society that weighs upon it. . . . Sublime love could not, in fact, admit of the least restriction: *all or nothing.*"[7]

The danger remains clear. As Mayoux says in his *Contre-Courant* article, "Too many obstacles oppose the search for and recognition of the other 'half'; too much fatigue undermines love and the power to love; too many men and women have to utter the despairing cry of Maiakovsky: 'The boat of love has been broken upon the tide of life'." Péret is not sentimentalizing when, in his anthology of sublime love, he declares woman beautiful to the extent that she "embodies more completely the secret aspirations of man, inciting him to turn full power over to his faculties of sublimation" (p. 70). Nor is Breton, when he announces in *Arcane 17* that "the great malediction is raised" and that "all the regenerative power of the world" resides in love (p. 78). Neither suggests the benefits of love come easily. Both are fully aware that these benefits have to be defended energetically, and sometimes against the most subtle temptations to be unfaithful to love.

Even after he has fallen in love, Parry still succumbs to temptation. He continues to seek approval from society, through continued efforts to establish his innocence. Allowing social norms to impose direction and limits on what he does, he comes close to letting society alone decide what "*qualifies*" him. In striving obstinately to prove himself worthy of reacceptance into society, Surrealists find, he displays a weakness to which Breton helps direct attention when pointing out in *Arcane 17* that man's greatest enemy is "opacity":

"This opacity is outside him and it is above all within him, maintained by conventional opinions and all sorts of suspect defenses" (p. 52).

So long as Parry acts quite conventionally—according to the commonly accepted principle that every innocent person has the right (not to say the obligation) to have his innocence acknowledged publicly—he has not yet grasped, as Péret obviously did, that love is asocial and sometimes even antisocial. According to Péret, if man is a social being, "social man opposes the human being, in proportion to the development of society that ceaselessly engenders new constraints" (p. 24). Finally, Vincent Parry comes to understand this, his discovery marking the end of an inner struggle that *Dark Passage* does not examine overtly. As Surrealists see it, his human qualities surface when he succeeds in detaching himself from dependence on society. His decision to run away is no sign of cowardice but full acknowledgment of what love demands and of what it gives in return.

Parry does not betray despair or even bitterness in turning his back on the world he has known. To the Surrealists, his decision to leave North America signals his realization that reciprocal love is, in the phrase Breton uses on one page of *Arcane 17*, "the only one to condition total magnetization that nothing can have a hold over" (p. 41).

One reason Vincent Parry's predicament commands the Surrealists' attention is that he has to struggle longer than Irene Jansen to come to full acknowledgment of love, to reach a point she attains much sooner than he. In Surrealism, woman—in the best possible sense a creature of love—is seen as mediating between man and the marvelous. Irene impeccably fills the role reserved for woman in the Surrealist myth of love which leads Robert Desnos to equate liberty and love in his novel *La Liberté ou l'amour!* (1927) and induces Paul Eluard to treat love and poetry as interchangeable terms in his verse collection *L'Amour la poésie* (1930).

As *Dark Passage* reaches its closing stages, Parry's actions show he has emerged into the light. They denote that he has ceased to be a mere social man. He is able at last to turn away from society because, recognizing in the end the self-sufficiency of love, he no longer depends on other people's approval to define and sustain his identity. Repudiation of societal obligations marks his unreserved commitment to love, which Surrealists unhesitatingly link with the cause of nonacceptance.

In his *Anthologie de l'Amour sublime* Benjamin Péret declares that all myths reflect "man's ambivalence toward the world and himself." He goes on to suggest that this ambivalence results from a "profound feeling of dissociation" inherent in human nature. Feeling his weakness under the natural forces weighing upon him, man nevertheless "has a presentiment that he might be able to live a less precarious existence and feel happier" (p. 19). There can be no doubt, then, why the Surrealists elaborated their myth of love. Defending them against an unnatural force, society, it has enabled them to surmount a sense of loss based in man's feeling of dissociation by offering the compensation of union with woman, in opposition to oppressive societal demands.

Now we see why Péret takes up the hackneyed phrase "the other half" that Jehan Mayoux is quite willing to use also. Péret stresses that, together, the couple forms a whole, completing "the magic operation" that, according to Marianne van Hirtum's definition of "meeting" in the *Lexique succinct de l'érotisme*, changes two separate persons into "one body with two heads" (p. 61). Parry's conduct—and Irene's willingness to fall in with his plans to meet in South America—demonstrates to the Surrealist that love, as Péret's anthology of sublime love puts it, "translates man's pressing appeal addressed to the being who embodies what he lacks to make an harmonious whole" (p. 71).

As we see the lovers, reunited in a distant country, dancing together perfectly content in one another's company and needing no words to express what they feel, a question still remains. Apparently, it goes unanswered. One may be willing enough to grant that Parry's supposedly escapist withdrawal from the world that unjustly condemned him is a liberative gesture of considerable emotional appeal. But, starting life over again, and in a country whose culture is different from their own, have Vincent Parry and Irene Jansen really gained anything? They have taken a great stride in their liberative struggle for freedom to live by love rather than at society's behest. Yet, actually, they have done no more, it seems, than exchange one form of society for another. They still will have

to make adjustments, will they not? Fortunately for the Surrealists—whose idealism is not different from Goodis's and
Daves's in this respect—*Dark Passage* comes to an end before
this question has to be faced. To anyone inclined to object that
the Surrealists' interpretation of the movie is invalidated
nevertheless, Breton's *Arcane 17* offers this riposte: "Rebel-
lion carries its own justification, quite independently of the
chances it has of modifying or not the state of affairs that gives
rise to it" (p. 154-55). Nothing can deter Surrealists from looking upon *Dark Passage* as a marvelous poetic statement of in-
finite resonance.

6

Albert Lewin:
Pandora and the Flying Dutchman
(1951)

THE FUNDAMENTAL FACT is still not as widely admitted as it should be that Surrealists regard cinema and look at films in a way peculiarly and revealingly their own. Yet it is scarcely an exaggeration to say that, until this is accepted as a truism, Surrealism's contribution to the film medium will not be understood fully, let alone evaluated accurately. It is not enough to treat Surrealists as somewhat strange people in whom curious tastes and beliefs often fire enthusiasm for movies that the rest of us—intelligent, sensitive theatergoers, needless to say—dismiss as of dubious quality or even as quite worthless. Surrealism is not merely an oddity, giving rise to a peculiar but entirely passive approach to cinema—a harmless subjective way of enjoying films that does not touch our own understanding of what cinema serves to accomplish and by which means, because it implicates no one but the Surrealist spectator himself. When it is the movie director who looks at the world from Surrealist perspective and sets out, accordingly, to make a film that presents reality from a Surrealist angle, then Surrealism fosters an active approach to movies. No member of the audience can mistake or ignore this without distorting both the film-maker's intentions and the way he attempts to achieve them.

Where purpose and accomplishment are misinterpreted or not given serious consideration, incomprehension takes its toll no less than active antagonism. Surrealism's presence in the cinema is denied a significance that fully deserves to be recognized. As a consequence, a movie of Surrealist inspiration comes to be regarded as an anomaly. Because its motivation eludes attention, the methods it brings into play inevitably are misunderstood. This is only to be expected, after all. Whatever

123

Ava Gardner and the ageless Pandora.

his medium of expression, the Surrealist artist's technical means are strictly subject to the demands made upon them by his own antiaesthetic ends. Thus when its central purpose escapes detection by an outsider, any Surrealist work risks appearing to be of questionable validity. One example will show well enough what results.

Admittedly, reporting on films currently playing in New York City, *The New Yorker* magazine has no space for delicately balanced judgments. Still, the tone of a notice appearing in its August 22, 1977 issue is unmistakably patronizing, and even implicitly hostile. Here a Hollywood movie, *Pandora and the Flying Dutchman* (1951), is described as "certifiably one of a kind." Readers are informed that Albert Lewin (who "wrote the screenplay, produced the film, and directed it too) "has more visual feeling than common sense." They are told in addition that his direction is "static" and his staging "so luxuriantly mad that it's easy to get fixated on what, if anything, he could have had in mind." This uncertain attempt to take out insurance against faulty judgment is followed by the more definite assertion that Sally Bowles might have called *Pandora and the Flying Dutchman* "divinely incoherent." Needless to say, Albert Lewin – producer in 1935 of an Academy Award winner, *Mutiny on the Bounty* – called his movie something else altogether. He put the whole matter beyond doubt when he explained, "Independently of the use I have made of it, in my films [*The Moon and Sixpence, The Picture of Dorian Gray, The Private Lives of Bel Ami* – the last occasioned a competition among a dozen painters, a number of them affiliated with Surrealism, all invited to paint a canvas on the theme of the temptation of Saint Anthony: Max Ernst was the winner], I have always been interested in painting of every style, and particularly in the Surrealists' works. . . . It was therefore, for me, natural to turn to make a deliberately Surrealist film. This desire took form in *Pandora*."[1] In *Pandora and the Flying Dutchman* cinematography by an excellent technician, Jack Cardiff, serves to capture the atmosphere of Surrealist painting, which Lewin not only admired but collected too.

The contrast is easy to see, when we turn from *The New Yorker*'s condescending notes, from *The Observer*'s review ("Conspicuous in its confident assumption of scholarship and in its utter poverty of taste and imagination"), or from the one appearing in *The Times* of London ("a script of incredible pretentiousness") to comments on *Pandora* by Surrealism's most voluble spokesman on cinema. In his *Amour-Erotisme et cinéma* (1966), Ado Kyrou cites this movie as having a place among "a few shooting stars leaving a dazzling trail" in the Hollywood film industry's treatment of love (p. 94). Soon he is speaking of Lewin's motion picture as "a luminous milestone" and is praising its heroine, Pandora Reynolds, as, "with Lya Lys (in *L'âge d'or*) the only wildly surrealist woman in any cinema" (p. 238).

It is debatable, of course, whether a few arch yet patently self-contradictory lines printed anonymously in a popular weekly magazine can be taken as representative of serious film criticism. All the same, the assurance with which *The New Yorker* ridicules Lewin for lack of common sense speaks for itself. So does the blackening deduction that, having little or nothing in mind, he perpetrated a reprehensibly incoherent movie, or (to quote the daily newspapers) a tasteless, unimaginative, and pretentious one. By the same token, Kyrou's habit of lavishing unstinting praise on every movie that appeals to him (and, presenting a bewildering array, there are so many films that do) suggests an unsettling absence of critical rigor. This surely must leave his readers hesitant, if not quite unconvinced at times. Whatever the intrinsic appeal of Josef von Sternberg's *Shanghai Express* (1932), for instance, one cannot but be suspicious of Kyrou's enthusiasm for this movie (a still from it decorates the cover of the 1957 edition of his *Amour-Erotisme et cinéma*) upon learning in his *Le Surréalisme au cinéma* (1963) that he came under its spell—more exactly under the spell of Marlene Dietrich in the role of Shanghai Lily—when he was no more than nine. Nevertheless, together with Lewin's statement of intent, Kyrou's unrestrained excitement over *Pandora and the Flying Dutchman* revealingly brings out nothing but total insensitivity on the other side, to which, by the way, belongs James Mason, who played the male lead in the film. It makes abundantly clear that a Surrealist and a nonSurrealist can look at the selfsame movie and not see the same thing at all. But this we already knew. There is still more to be learned from examining Lewin's film.

Whereas in movies emanating from Hollywood we expect to find any Surrealist elements present to be only implicit, beyond the directors' ken as well as outside their interest, we face something unique in *Pandora*. One cannot assess this film fairly and accurately without taking account of the frame of mind in which Lewin wrote and then assumed the task of directing his screenplay. The Surrealist effect achieved in this movie reflects conscious purpose, not mere accident or coincidence. Hence a Surrealist reading of *Pandora and the Flying Dutchman* is not simply permissible; it is openly and actively solicited through every aspect of film production.

One cannot give Lewin's movie its true worth without being mindful of René Crevel's words: "The poet does not put his wild animals to sleep to play the animal trainer, but, with all cages open, the keys thrown to the wind, he sets off, a voyager who does not think of himself but of the voyage, of beaches dreamed about, forests of hands, animals of souls, of all undeniable surreality." So long as Lewin is granted the status of poet which, in Surrealist eyes, he earns for himself in *Pandora*, Paul Eluard's remark is equally relevant: "For it is hope or despair that will determine for the wide-awake sleeper—for the poet—the action of his imagination. Let him only formulate that hope or despair and his relations with the world will change immediately. . . . All that is concrete then becomes food for his imagination . . . ."

Pandora and the Flying Dutchman is not the freakish example of craziness *The New Yorker*'s critic takes it to be. Written, produced, and directed in Hollywood, it was intended to bring Surrealism to the screen in defiance of Hollywood practice. Thus it is evident that, in one very important respect, Albert Lewin had to approach film-making in 1951 much as Luis Buñuel did during the years when, after leaving Europe (with *Un Chien andalou, L'Age d'Or,* and *Las Hurdes* all behind him), he was obliged to submit to the inescapable restrictions of commercialism. To a noteworthy degree, *Pandora and the Flying Dutchman* was composed by images. Hence, while following his story line with the utmost fidelity, Lewin handled plot the way Buñuel did, in an oft-repeated gesture of self-respect. Lewin treated narrative as the occasion (at times, one could even say as an excuse) for bringing before his audience certain scenes of special visual impact. As in Buñuel's commercial movies, such scenes stand out and cannot be ignored, even when they are totally misunderstood. Because their presence does not always seem to have been imposed by the strict requirements of plot development, to many a viewer they sometimes look more or less extraneous. For this reason, some members of the public take them to be indicative of directorial waywardness, of weakness, or of a self-indulgence they find hard to explain and no less difficult to condone.

Looking back to the time when he was making *Los Olvidados* (1950) in Mexico, Buñuel once recalled, "Into the most realistic scenes, I wanted to introduce some mad, completely disparate elements. For instance, when Jaibo is going to beat up and kill the other boy [Pedro], a camera shift reveals, in the distance, the framework of a high eleven-story building under construction. I wanted to put an orchestra with a hundred musicians in that building. One would have seen it in passing, vaguely. I wanted to put in many elements of that kind, but it was absolutely forbidden."[2] Enjoying greater independence of action while filming *Pandora* the following year, Lewin was able to set up and shoot a number of comparable images. If these are likely to disconcert the movie theater audience somewhat, it is not because they are demonstrably more acceptable to common sense. The public is less disinclined to pass over them, rather, because they present themselves in a film that appears more suited to accommodating the fanciful than Buñuel's grim story of slum life in Mexico, which won the Official Jury Prize for best direction at the 1951 Cannes Festival. In fact, it is not intent that makes the difference, here, but receptivity on the spectator's part.

As utilized to Surrealist effect by Buñuel and Lewin, the technique of composition by images is essentially an act of deliberate provocation. Both directors know that the response elicited by what they show on film will divide those with whom each of them aims and manages to communicate his *"vision surréaliste"* from those to whom he has nothing really important to say. While he was shooting *Los Olvidados*, devotion to the cause of Surrealism brought a form of censorship down on Buñuel. To Lewin it brought an equally sure sign of incomprehension for *Pandora and the Flying Dutchman*: mockery.

Albert Lewin was to single out two episodes which, having

Credit: Bill O'Connell

The transitory balanced by the timeless. The incongruous bathing suit is framed between the male dancer's formal attire and two archeological artifacts, unaccountably standing upright like the Greek columns.

puzzled his financial backers, came close to being excised from *Pandora*. One shows men wearing tuxedos dancing on a beach with women in swimsuits, to the tune *You're Driving Me Crazy*, played by a jazz combo placed "in an erotic way" among pieces of statuary, with the sea as backdrop to the scene. Recalling that he had been expected to leave this sequence out, on the pretext that it had nothing to do with his story, Lewin commented, "Maybe the sculptures in Chartres Cathedral ought to be taken out, since the building would stand up without them" (p. 169). The second episode presents an attempt on the land speed record. The latter is undertaken by Pandora's fiancé, pricked by jealousy of her former lover, a bullfighter who has just given a spectacular demonstration of his professional skill. Lewin describes the scene as "a meteor passing at high speed in front of the statue of a Greek goddess, upright in the sand." Again, his backers asked him to cut; this time not only because the scene contributed nothing they found important to the plot but also because it was difficult (and, it goes without saying, expensive) to shoot. "And yet the fact of eliminating that scene would have spoiled my ambi-

tions and reduced to nothing what I had to say, in making this
film."

Albert Lewin saw no reason to hide what had inspired the
scene in question, and indeed his film *Pandora* as a whole. He
admitted to having been especially excited by a habit of jux-
taposing the old and the new he had noticed among Surrealist
painters (the examples he cited were Giorgio de Chirico and
Paul Delvaux, both of whom make extensive use of statuary in
their canvases). As he took care to stress, in his movie the figure of the Flying Dutchman symbolizes that same juxtaposition of past and present. Hence, far from being superfluous,
the car racing on the beach actually was the first image to form
in his mind. It was the one, he insisted, that had impelled him
to develop the story of *Pandora and the Flying Dutchman* in
the first place.

We cannot be sure what it was, exactly, that prompted
Lewin to give his screenplay the direction it took. All the
same, the following extract from a text that could well have
held his attention, given his predisposition toward Surrealism—an interview André Breton granted Charles-Henri
Ford for the special Surrealism number of *View* (No. 7-8,
October-November 1941), where it appeared in English—reads like a commentary on *Pandora* no less than as a
succinct summary of Surrealist principles: "Surrealism, as you
know, has always endeavored to answer to two sorts of preoccupations, the first arising from the *eternal* (the mind grappl-
ing with the state of man) and the other arising from the *actual*
(the mind witness of its own movement. For this movement to
have any value, we maintain that *in reality as in dream* the
mind must go beyond the 'manifest content' of events to arrive
at the consciousness of their 'latent content')."

The first time the Dutchman Hendrick van der Zee appears
before us—and this, naturally, is something Lewin takes care
to emphasize in his published comments on *Pandora and the
Flying Dutchman*—he is painting a portrait for which he has
no model before him: presumably, then, the portrait of someone he does not have to see in order to paint. Swimming nude
out to his ship, anchored in the bay, Pandora arrives aboard to
discover her own features delineated in the picture. How

could she know that she looks exactly like the woman to whom the artist was married, hundreds of years before?

As a frustrating negative force, time appears to all Surrealists the way Breton once described it, as "an old sinister farce, a train perpetually running off the rails, a mad pulsation, an inextricable heap of animals dead and dying." But, at the moment of Pandora's meeting with the Flying Dutchman, *l'éternel* becomes one with *l'actuel* (in its sense of "present" as well as "actual"). As Lewin emphasizes, van der Zee takes on a "purely surrealist aspect," when his desire for love brings Pandora to him and a gap in time is bridged. Now we see time begin functioning positively, unhampered by chronology because it is vitally responsive to human need, not to clock and calendar. This is one of those "explosions of time" that, according to Paul Eluard, are "ever-ripe fruit for memory."

Over the years, we are reminded, magazines edited by participants in Surrealism have testified enthusiastically to their keen interest in strange incidents, in inexplicable coincidences and parallels, in predictions that history has proved to be uncannily accurate, and in other evidence they find supportive of their view that we only limit ourselves by submitting to the disheartening idea that time is an external force by which everyone is imprisoned without hope of escape. It is not simply weakness for the fanciful, then, but a deep-seated urge to believe time need not be our enemy that leads Surrealists to give *Pandora and the Flying Dutchman* the attention Lewin hoped his movie would receive. In their minds, his adaptation of the Flying Dutchman legend has no other value (and requires none) than to dispose of temporal limitations, as love intervenes in life to confer the fulfillment that comes through liberation. Retold by Albert Lewin, the story of the Flying Dutchman gives Surrealist coloration to the word "legend." It bears out Georges Hugnet's remark, "A legend you were saying? No—rather a found object of which the geranium is the buckler and the domino the mouth." In its own way, *Pandora and the Flying Dutchman* reiterates a lyrical declaration from André Breton's *Point du jour* [Break of day (1934)]: "There is no solution outside love" (p. 75).

According to Salvador Dalí, "Everything leads us to think that love is only a sort of incarnation of the dreams corroborating the standard phrase that says a woman loved is a dream become flesh and blood." The originality of *Pandora and the Flying Dutchman* lies, in other words, in showing the reciprocal satisfaction of love. In the person of a flesh-and-blood woman, beneficent chance (which sends him his wife reincarnated as Pandora Reynolds) provides the Dutchman with the object of desire made immortal in a timeless world we would call unreal. Meanwhile Pandora finds in van der Zee fulfillment of desires which neither her lover nor her fiancé has been able to meet.

In *Ajours*, which appeared in 1947, André Breton spoke of devoting oneself to love just as he did of devoting oneself to painting or poetry. He pronounced love valid when it means *"entering into a trance"* (p. 206). Does Lewin try to intimate something similar? To many people it must seem that *Pandora and the Flying Dutchman* does not merely draw us to the border of whimsy but transports us, as in a trance, into the world of the fantastic. Some of these will argue confidently that, so long as we are dealing with Surrealism, this is only to be expected. They will quote the well-known footnote on the first Surrealist manifesto where Breton assures his readers, "What is admirable in the fantastic is that there is no fantastic any more; there is only the real."[3] However, in the long run the supposition that, for Surrealists, the fantastic is reality itself can be misleading, no less so than the popular belief that Surrealism is present, somewhere, in everything unusual enough to stand outside familiar experience.

It is significant that the 1924 *Manifeste du surréalisme* does not extol the fantastic per se. Nor does it propose the fantastic as an admirable ideal that assuredly will oust the real. It certainly does not promise that Surrealists in all corners of the globe will hold themselves ready to admire the fantastic without reservation, whenever and wherever it should happen to manifest itself. Breton's meaning becomes clearer only as analysis of his statement brings the following to light. The fantastic stimulates Surrealists to admiration when and where it has ceased to be identifiable solely with the exceptional, with what we are unable to accept as real. It provokes their admiration when it shows that the vulgar realism to which Buñuel's superiors would have liked to see him limit himself in *Los Olvidados* can be surpassed. How to challenge the reality principle without stepping outside the real? This problem

Luis Buñuel solved by introducing into his movie elements taken straight out of reality that seemingly do not belong by right to the world we call real. The result is thoroughly disturbing when, for example, we are made to look at a legless cripple wriggling on the sidewalk like some monstrous oversized enraged insect, after a street gang has tipped him out of the wooden trolley in which he pushes himself around the neighborhood by his arms.

Less brutally shocking, less sensational, certainly—and this, one might say, is to Lewin's credit—is the final shot in *Pandora and the Flying Dutchman*. Given prominence by Kyrou, as might be expected (and in both his books, incidentally), it shows the lovers' drowned bodies, brought up out of the sea in a fishing net. This incontestably realistic detail that might have produced a grisly effect introduces, instead, a potent film image. The latter lets us see that the lovers' clasped hands cannot be separated. At the end of the movie it provides a definitive affirmation of the reality of a love affair the audience has considered it fitting to term fantastic. The real and the fantastic have become one; admirably so, Breton would have said. For it is no longer possible to distinguish between them.

If it seems too far-fetched to suggest that our sense of what is real now has changed appreciably, this is because the objections surfacing in our minds arise in active protest against something common sense assures us cannot be true. Rationality may well reassert its claims when the film is over, determined to discredit everything Lewin has worked to bring before us. But it can do so only retrospectively, in a self-defensive reflex against a statement that reason has found unacceptable and hence inadmissible. Before this can happen, though, in the moment of experiencing the visual image of a man (a ghost) and a (real) woman joined in death, we make contact with Surrealism. The latter comes to us in its unadulterated state because our eyes stimulate our imagination to activity of a kind in which reason has no part to play. In fact, reason is powerless to intervene at the moment when the scene makes its visual impact. In other words, C. A. Lejeune's complaint in *The Observer* about the poverty of imagination displayed in *Pandora* is surely the most unjust criticism ever made of the movie and obviously reveals much about the condition of its author's own imagination.

Pandora and the Flying Dutchman tells a story in which time plays a central role. The action is set in a little Spanish coastal village, appropriately called Esperanza. In the bay lies a ship on which no crew is ever visible. Aboard is its owner, the legendary Dutchman. Under a curse for having killed his wife whom he suspected of infidelity centuries before, every seventh year he is permitted to spend six months in the company of other men. He comes ashore to seek a woman who will consent to sacrifice her life to her love for him, so releasing him from the fate of endlessly roaming the seas.

To the extent that Albert Lewin's movie is overtly faithful to the tenets of Surrealism, it can leave no doubt at all about one thing. As Breton put it in his *Second Manifeste du sur-réalisme*, originally published in 1929, Surrealists are quite willing to be considered "the tail" of romanticism. At the same time, *Pandora* displays enough originality to vindicate Breton's clear specification, *"but then such a prehensile tail"* (p. 184).

For one thing, as a director, Lewin is working with his own material, bringing to the screen subject matter about which he has no reservations or misgivings of any kind. He does not have to exercise ingenuity or resort to guile, like Buñuel on more than one occasion, in order to leave his special mark on a film for which others have provided the theme and the basic ingredients. This man who, in the past, has been resigned to reserving no more than fifteen minutes or so for himself in the films entrusted to his direction is undeterred, now, by the fact that his screenplay for *Pandora* will not only be dubbed romantic, in the pejorative sense of the word, but will strike rational-minded people as implausible, as quite incredible, in fact. Believing in what he has to say, the producer-director-writer of *Pandora and the Flying Dutchman*, for whom this movie is a forthright statement of faith in Surrealism, sees no necessity to prepare for any attack by donning the armor of irony or self-protective humor. He follows his hero's adventures with utter seriousness.

Never for an instant does Lewin waver in treating Hendrick

van der Zee's predicament as agonizing. And without a hint of
equivocation he demonstrates that salvation does not come to
the Dutchman through divine forgiveness (in which Surrealists have no belief), as it does to Eugène Sue's Wandering
Jew, who has had more than one incarnation in the cinema. It
comes, just as Surrealism teaches it can do, through the redemptive love of a woman. In other words, Albert Lewin radically modifies his mythical source material.

In Greek myth, the reign of Cronus was a time when gods
and men lived on terms of mutual understanding. *The
Theogony* of Hesiod tells us, "In those days meals were taken
in common; men and the immortal gods sat down together."
Everything changed, however, with the arrival of the Olym-
pians and with Zeus's assertion of his divine supremacy over
mankind. Outrage at Prometheus's theft of fire led Zeus, now
bent on punishing men, to order Hephaestus—to whom nothing was impossible—to fashion from clay and water a virgin
whose beauty would equal that of the immortal goddesses.
The Horae having embellished her hair with floral garlands
and Hermes having put perfidy in her heart and lies in her
mouth, this first woman, called Pandora, was received among
men. She arrived bearing an enormous vase from which terrible afflictions were released on the world, only hope remaining.

Changing this myth pattern, and coincidentally denying the
biblical version of the first woman's role in the fall of man,
Lewin practices the kind of modification that Péret considered a "rectification" of the universe, carried out, as Surrealism demands, to the satisfaction of human desire. Thus, in
this movie so often filmed against the statues of Greek gods
and goddesses, Pandora Reynolds becomes salvation in
human form, not perdition. And she exercises her power for
the benefit of a man whom release from the bonds of time,
visited upon him as a punishment, has made quasi-divine.

In Lewin's film the role of Pandora (who, early on, watches
without emotion as a playboy commits suicide out of love for
her) falls to Ava Gardner. What does it matter that this actress
consistently calls a poem a "pome"? Her carnal attractions
draw from Kyrou, in *Amour-Erotisme et cinéma,* the remark
that she is "beautiful as a statue about to come to life, a tree on
fire, a desire realized" (p. 294). Although critics may cavil, the

Pandora and the Flying Dutchman; (top), facing his painting of her mythological namesake; (bottom), with an hourglass, acting out a "pome."

public has responded to the sincerity with which Albert Lewin has brought a familiar legend to life by infusing it with Surrealist meaning.

In *Pandora and the Flying Dutchman* the barrier cutting the fantastic off from the real has disappeared. True to Surrealist principles, the movie's director does not regard their separation as important enough to warrant his attention or his audience's. In this respect Lewin places complete trust in his public, as he does, too, when he denies the viability of the common assumption that the world generally called real exists apart from and distinct from the oneiric domain. After his escape from prison, van der Zee is seen awaiting death for the murder of his young wife. He now has a dream during which he picks up a dagger and tries to kill himself. Unable to commit suicide, he lets the weapon fall to the floor. Upon rewakening, he sees the very same dagger lying exactly where he dropped it in his dream. Thus the waking state, as René Crevel would put it, "has ceased to discomfit dreaming." Moreover, like the Dutchman himself, the audience is offered no alternative but to accept the unification of dreaming and waking experience. Like his, their eyes have reported that, in *Pandora and the Flying Dutchman*, dream infringes upon the world of the real, becoming one with it.

The dream involving a dagger and the prolongation of that dream into the world of reality formulate with particular clarity the idea of confronting contrasts upon which Lewin's movie is built. As he has intimated, the modern racing car rushing at speed past an ancient statue (its immobility accentuated by its location, imbedded in sand) is only the starting point for *Pandora*. Similar oppositions recur everywhere in the film. They are emphasized by a directing style that has been interpreted, mistakenly, as static because Lewin pauses to dwell on significant contrasts. Evidently he aims, at least part of the time, to recreate the effect achieved by Delvaux, in whose painting tension often is heightened when action is suspended, just as in a film momentarily halted.

Lewin's staging is no less luxuriant than *The New Yorker* says it is. But to call it "mad" is to miss the point entirely, as well as its underlying motivation. Camera shots are elaborated with care. Despite the fact that the basic rules of cinematic composition rest upon the supposition that incongruent elements are best kept apart, Lewin stresses their simultaneous appearance. His purpose is not only to bring these together but to reconcile them. For it is the union of opposites, on the plane of desire realized, that he seeks to bring to our attention, in fullest agreement with the Surrealist theme of his movie.

A typical shot lets us observe van der Zee, his back to the camera, standing on a wooden jetty facing Pandora. Behind her, in the distance, rises a hill on which nothing much can be distinguished in the darkness. To the right, before another hill rises out of frame, is the village of Esperanza. Closer to us are fishing boats drawn up on the sand. In the foreground where one cannot fail to notice them, and as near as Pandora, two cars stand against the jetty steps. By all professional standards a compositional error, supposedly the result of negligence, the intrusion of these reminders of modern technology is no more accidental than the presence of the stone statue in another sequence, where its head and upper body are large enough to dwarf Pandora.

The episode with the dagger is only one of those highlighted by Lewin for their "obviously surrealist character." Another comes in the very next sequence. This one might be taken for the enactment of a dream. It is nothing of the kind, however. Showing the Flying Dutchman aboard his vessel, with the crew obeying orders he does not have to put into words, the scene has an effect that its director openly termed poetic and gladly attributed to Surrealist inspiration.

It would be an error to suppose that Albert Lewin wished to set magical events aboard the ship (from which, periodically, the magic number seven releases the Dutchman) systematically apart from what takes place in Esperanza. True, life ashore seems to proceed according to our expectations regarding normal life for the monied classes in the world of today. At any moment, though, the unexpected may intervene. When this occurs, it is with a logic that reminds us how limited is our understanding of what deserves to be called real.

On account of his knowledge of Dutch, Hendrick van der Zee is asked to translate an old manuscript, written in that language. The material proves to be the Flying Dutchman's diary, written many years before. What could be more natural, then, than that this man, who lives in the contingent but without a

sense of time, to the astonishment of his host should be trans-
lating from memory, without even glancing at the text? The
past has intruded on the present and the familiar surroundings
of the host's comfortable modern-day study fade into unimpor-
tance.

Van der Zee's host will never grasp the significance of what
he has witnessed. Even if he were to be given an explanation,
common sense would stand between him and its acceptance.
He then would find himself in the position of those who scoff
at *Pandora*, so betraying the self-righteousness of people in
whom reason cultivates intolerance of anything that dares to
flout rationality. The best to be hoped of him is that he will
look upon the incident as quite mysterious. Yet to those watching *Pandora and the Flying Dutchman* as Lewin means us to
watch, the key to the action is not mystery, which cries out for
elucidation. It is the marvelous, which transcends rational explanation and which André Breton opposed to the mysterious
in an essay from the ninth number of *Minotaure* (1936) reprinted in his *La Clé des champs* (1953). Erecting his plot on a
premise that reason will not support, Lewin makes no attempt
to adjust the marvelous to the requirements of rationality. Had
he wished to do this, in a gesture aimed at placating common
sense, he would have avoided closing his film with the union
of irreconcilables on the plane of marvelous coincidence and
with the resolution of apparent contradictions: past and present, eternal and transitory, possible and impossible.

With the final shot of his movie Albert Lewin openly ac-
knowledges that he is in full agreement with one of the central
ideas that nourish Surrealist imagery, in its verbal and pictorial forms no less than in the cinema. As formulated by Breton
in his second manifesto, this fundamental idea is a challenge
to the "old antinomies destined hypocritically to forestall any
unwonted agitation on man's part" (p. 153). "Everything,"
Breton declares, "leads us to believe there exists a certain
point of the mind from which life and death, real and imaginary, past and future, communicable and uncommunicable,
high and low cease to be perceived in contradiction" (p. 154).

The *Second Manifeste du surréalisme* has introduced a
theme that will recur often enough in Breton's writings, and
over a long enough period of time, to impress upon his readers
its fundamental importance in Surrealist thought. In *Les Vases*

communicants (1932) Breton will confide, apropos of Surrealism, "I hope it will be credited with having attempted nothing better than streching a conducting thread between the altogether too dissociated worlds of waking and sleeping, of external and internal reality . . ." (p. 101). In his lecture *Limites non frontières du surréalisme*, delivered in London in 1936 on the occasion of the International Surrealist Exhibition held in that city, he will speak again of the hope of resolving antinomies: "These antinomies are those of waking and sleeping (of reality and of dream), reason and madness, objective and subjective, perception and representation, past and future, the collective sense and love, life and death themselves." And addressing students at Yale University in December 1942, he will declare, "For surrealism—and I consider that this one day will be its glory—everything will have served to reduce those oppositions wrongly presented as insurmountable, deplorably marked out over the ages, that are the real alembics of suffering: the opposition of madness to so-called 'reason' that refuses to take the irrational into consideration, the opposition of dream and 'action' that believes it can impose inanity on dreaming . . . ."

Whether or not Albert Lewin was acquainted with these statements, there is no doubt at all on one score. He grasped the basic fact that, as Breton writes on the first page on his 1929 manifesto, Surrealism tends to provoke "a *crisis of consciousness* of the most general and most serious kind" (p. 153). The precise nature of that crisis eludes close definition, just as Surrealism itself does. Indeed, in this connection it is imperative to take into account the state of mind in which Louis Aragon likened Surrealism to the horizon line that retreats as one advances in its direction. Nevertheless, at the same time we must acknowledge something else too. As Breton insists when referring to the point in the mind where contradictions are subsumed in new awareness, it is fruitless to look behind Surrealist activities for any motivation other than "the hope of determining that point." Putting Breton's statement next to Aragon's brings to light yet another contradiction, one that shows how pressing is the crisis of consciousness produced by Surrealism. It brings into focus the central question raised in *Pandora and the Flying Dutchman*, as posed in Breton's second manifesto: "What in fact can be expected of the Surrealist experience by those who retain some concern for the place they occupy *in the world?*" (p. 154).

If *Pandora* is a genuine Surrealist work, this is not merely because its author-director dabbles casually in the fantastic as he offers an hour and a half of escapism to distract us from our daily cares. Lewin's film conducts us into "that mental place" to which the *Second Manifeste du surréalisme* alludes, the place "from which one cannot undertake any longer, except for oneself, a perilous but, we think, a final reconnaissance" (p. 154).

Like *Pandora and the Flying Dutchman*, Breton's text makes pointed reference to the full potential of the Surrealist venture. But it hints also at certain limitations. These are imposed not so much by the ambitions Surrealism instills as by the individual's capacity for pursuing Surrealism's aims energetically and profitably. Under the circumstances, the most Albert Lewin can do, when making a film in the spirit of Surrealism, is invite his audience into a place from which each of them has to accept, for himself or herself, the mental risk of embarking on a reconnaissance sortie in the direction of the horizon where the Surreal entices us onward.

7

Charles Laughton:
The Night of the Hunter (1955)

WHEN THE STORY TOLD in *Pandora and the Flying Dutchman* or *Peter Ibbetson*, or even *Dark Passage* is examined from the standpoint adopted by the Surrealists, it may seem, upon reflection, to depict a fairytale world of wish fulfillment. Here the intrusive realities of normal existence are kept at a safe distance. It appears, then, that Vincent Parry, Peter Ibbetson, and Hendrick van der Zee are all fortunate indeed to be protected, by the magic charm of love, from the menace infusing modern living with anxiety. The danger, now, is that anyone inclined to treat the Surrealist attitude toward love as no more than definitive proof of the presence of latter-day romantics among us is likely to associate the theme of redemptive love in Surrealism with some irresistible instinct for escapism, presumably underlying Surrealist thought and diverting it from the problems of day-to-day survival. The error into which he falls can be corrected most quickly, perhaps, if he gives his attention to the fascination terror holds for Surrealists.

The distinction between films of terror and those identified by the more popular designation "horror movies" is sufficiently important, here, to warrant emphasis. Surrealists have paid respect to a number of motion pictures commonly classified as horror movies. The work of James Whale, Tod Browning, and Roger Corman comes to mind, as does Riccardo Freda's and Mario Bava's. But the Surrealists' stress on terror indicates interest in something other than revulsion or shock before what the camera reveals. It points instead to the capacity possessed by films of terror to involve their audience in an emotion to which Surrealists attribute special benefits. In this regard, Browning's remarkable *Freaks* (1932), for so

143

The hunter pursues his terrified prey.

long banned, illustrates the appeal of horror movies when it submits us to the spectacle of an assortment of deformed human beings, employed as circus sideshow attractions—the human torso who lights his cigarettes with his mouth, for instance. At the same time, it transcends the limitations of the horror genre by involving us in the emotion of terror, when these people band together to take vengeance on a woman trapeze artist, whom they transform with knives and other frightening instruments into a monstrosity, a kind of human chicken, comparable to the human caimen who tells his story in André Pieyre de Mandiargues's tale *Le Passage Pommeraye*.[1]

A glance over the evidence that began building up when Surrealists first started publishing their opinions on cinema reveals an interesting fact. Among the earliest Surrealists, only films of terror could compete in popularity with slapstick comedies. Prominent among the first movies to persuade members of the Surrealist group that cinema was a medium well deserving of their notice were Robert Wiene's *Das Kabinett des Dr. Caligari* (1919) and F. W. Murnau's *Nosferatu, eine Symphonie des Grauens*. In *Le Journal littéraire* for January 31, 1925, Robert Desnos lauded Wiene's film as "one of those in which emotion comes closest to terror." In *Le Soir* on May 21, 1927, he was to observe that, in Murnau's, "Everything was sacrificed to poetry and nothing to art."

Reflecting a preference for poetry over artistry that is characteristic of the Surrealists' sense of values, Desnos's comments on *Nosferatu* remain vague all the same. For elucidation of the meaning he attached to "poetry" we have to turn to a remark published a little earlier, in the same newspaper. Discussing "*Cinéma frénétique et cinéma académique*," Desnos asserted in *Le Soir* on May 5, 1927, that talking of cinema entails dealing with "the links binding it to the solemn element of disquiet." In human life, to the Surrealists, the compensation brought by love seems no less valuable than its disruptive influence. Disruption, meanwhile, is complemented by disquiet. For the latter is seen as equally potent in releasing poetry by fostering rejection of the "summary realities" ridiculed by Jehan Mayoux as the province of unattractive "vulgar realism."

Terror commands the Surrealists' attention wherever, in

creative activity, it opposes vulgar realism. Discussing the kind of story she had tried to write, Clara Reeves spoke in the preface to her romance *The Old English Baron* of "a sufficient degree of the marvellous to excite the attention; enough of the manners of real life, to give air of probability to the work; and enough of the pathetic, to engage the heart in its behalf." In doing so, she pointed to the elements in English Gothic romance that have attracted the Surrealists' notice as poetic and thus have elicited their praise—from Breton and Péret, for instance.

This is not the place to ask why Surrealists so admire Gothic novels. We may note, however, that parallels do exist between typical features of the Gothic mode and Surrealism. Buñuel worked with Jean-Claude Carrière on a screenplay adapted from Matthew Gregory Lewis's *The Monk*, publishing it in Jean Schuster's *"Le Désordre"* series in 1971, before it was brought to the screen by Ado Kyrou in 1972. The important thing, really, is that characteristics appealing to the Surrealist imagination in Gothic romance distinguish, also, films of terror in which Surrealists find something of true and lasting value. In his article on *"Cinéma frénétique et cinéma académique,"* Desnos attempted to render an atmosphere that Surrealists are bound to consider propitious:

Lost in a deep forest, whose floor is made of moss and pine needles and where the light, filtered by high eucalyptus trees with hanging bark, by pines as green as the meadows promised the souls of good free wild horses, by oaks with knotty bodies tortured by infernal maladies, sometimes is yellow like dead leaves, sometimes white like the edge of woods, the modern traveler seeks the marvelous. He seems to recognize his route by feeling his way. He seems to recognize the domain promised his dreams by night. Night falls thick and full of mysteries and promises. A great searchlight pursues fabulous creatures. Here is Nosferatu the Vampire; here is the asylum where Cesare and Dr. Caligari met memorable adventures; here, rising up from poetic caverns, are Jack the Ripper, Yvan the Terrible and their old friend from *Waxworks*.

Desnos's last reference is to the film *Das Wachsenfiguren Kabinett* made in 1924 by Paul Leni, whose Hollywood movies *The Cat and the Canary* (1927) and *The Last Warning* (1929) are much admired by Ado Kyrou. In his *Le Surréalisme au cinéma* (1963), Kyrou declares that Leni has defined "the possibilities of terror in cinema." For in Paul Leni's films, portraits with human eyes, hands that appear from behind curtains, cobwebbed corridors, and strange apparitions "open the door on the poetry of fear" (p. 89).

This phrase defines as well as any the kind of poetry Surrealists discover in films of terror. It establishes a close link between the Surrealist outlook on cinema and a movie that Kyrou finds to be "a veritable surrealist poem" (p. 203), Charles Laughton's *The Night of the Hunter* (1955).

As the only complete film directed by an Academy Award-winning actor of enviable reputation, *The Night of the Hunter* is a unique work. Made with flair and a sense of atmosphere that bears witness to a grasp of cinematic technique and a feeling for form that even Kyrou cannot ignore or ridicule, it is an exceptional study in movie terror. It draws strength from camera work by Stanley Cortez, who photographed Orson Welles's *The Magnificent Ambersons* (1942), and from a thoroughly competent screenplay adapted in 1954 from a novel by Davis Grubb by no less a writer than James Agee, who died before this film was completed and whose *A Death in the Family* won a Pulitzer Prize in 1958. In form and substance, it explores the phenomenon of terror by adopting—without condescension or compromise—the viewpoint of the very young.

The result is an experiment in cinematic form fully deserving of note as exemplifying the *"vision surréaliste,"* to borrow a phrase used by Louis Buñuel when speaking of his Surrealist way of looking at things through film.

The Night of the Hunter is worthy of a place next to a select number of movies in which terror creates a frenetic atmosphere, films like Michael Powell's *The Peeping Tom* (1958), Georges Franju's *Les Yeux sans visage* (1959), and *L'Oribile Segreto del Dottor Hichcock* [*The Horrible Dr. Hichcock*] made in 1962 by Riccardo Freda, using the pseudonym Robert Hampton. Reviewing this last film, which he called "a hymn to necrophilia," Gérard Legrand took care to insist that Dr. Hichcock is possessed by "a mysterious passion of a type far more oneiric than morbid." The passion ruling Harry Powell's life in *The Night of the Hunter* warrants the same comment.

In André Breton's first Surrealist manifesto of 1924 we read,

"I believe in the future resolution of those two states, apparently so contradictory, of dream and reality, in a sort of absolute reality, of *surreality* if one may call it so."[2] Laughton's realistic tale of terror has a dream quality to which our attention is directed even before the action begins. While the titles are running, we hear a lullaby that repeats the words, "Dream, little one, dream./Dream, my little one, dream." It is not long before we have realized the ironic force of these lyrics. At one dramatically tense moment, for example, as in a nightmare, movement slows down, when the film's children, John and Pearl Harper, are trying to reach a small boat in which they hope to float downstream and escape from their murderous stepfather, Harry Powell.

John is nine years old. His sister, inseparable from a rag doll called Miss Jenny, is no more than five. They live in a small rural community with their parents. Driven to despair by the Depression, Ben Harper holds up a bank, killing two men while stealing close to ten thousand dollars with which he returns home, just ahead of the state police. He hides the money (in the doll, we discover after a while), making his children swear never to reveal its whereabouts.

Awaiting execution after being condemned to death, Ben meets another prisoner, Harry Powell. Hearing about the money but unable to find out where it is concealed, the latter heads, upon his release, for the one-street town on the Ohio River where Willa Harper still lives with John and Pearl. He and Willa marry.

When the children's mother at last realizes Powell lied, telling her Ben had confided in him that the stolen money is at the bottom of the river, Powell kills her. During the night, he drives her body off the river bank in Harper's Model-T Ford. Then he spreads the word that she deserted him. "She'll not be back. I reckon I'm safe in promisin' you that!"[3] Now, he says, he intends to assume the burden of raising the children all on his own.

Willa's body is discovered by the children's uncle, Birdie Steptoe, who will describe later how her hair looked in the river current, "wavin' soft and lazy like meadow grass under flood water, and that slit in her throat like she had an extry mouth." As Birdie looks down in horror from his fishing skiff, we hear Powell's voice singing a favorite hymn: "Leaning,

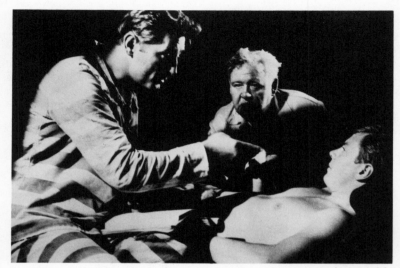

Credit: Cinemabilia

Expressionistic publicity shot of Charles Laughton directing the prison sequence. Robert Mitchum has the script in his lap.

leaning / Safe and secure from all alarms. / Leaning, leaning, / Leaning on the Everlasting Arms." Before he has finished singing, the camera has cut to the yard outside the Harper home. Powell is leaning against a tree. He calls seductively, "Children! Children?" As he walks toward the house an iris lens closure directs our attention to the cellar window, behind which John and Pearl can be seen watching apprehensively.

Earlier signs of Powell's cruelty (at one moment he threatened to tear Pearl's arm off, if she would not tell) are confirmed, now that the children have no one to protect them from his ruthless determination to force them to say where the money is. Hoping to make them speak up, he deprives them of supper. Still Pearl will not speak, because John has told her not to. Powell produces the switch-blade he used to cut their mother's throat. "Looky here," he says to Pearl. "You know what *that* is? Want to see something cute? Now looky." The knife springs open. "How about *that*? That's what I use on meddlers. *John* might be a meddler." he frightens the little girl so much that John volunteers to show where the money is concealed—in the cellar, he says.

Having managed to lock their stepfather in the cellar, the children run off to Uncle Birdie who has promised they can always turn to him for help. They find that the old man, fearing he will be accused of murdering their mother, has drunk himself into a stupor. "There's still the river," says John. They launch their father's skiff, recently repaired by Birdie, and head downriver, pursued by Powell on a horse for which he has cut a farmer's throat. To the sound of the lullaby we heard during the titles, John and Pearl come ashore after dark, to hide in a stable loft: "Rest, little one, rest." As the song draws to an end, dogs start barking. Then Powell's voice can be heard, singing: "What a fellowship,/What a peace is mine,/Leaning on the Everlasting Arms./What a blessedness,/What a joy is mine,/Leaning on the Everlasting Arms." We can see Powell, now, silhouetted on the skyline, astride the stolen horse. His relentless persistence and unerring sense of direction make it clear that the children have not escaped from their nightmare after all. "Don't he *never* sleep?" John wonders aloud. He rouses Pearl and, in the middle of the night, they take to the water again.

At last they find refuge with Rachel Cooper, who takes in and cares for homeless children. Meanwhile, displaying uncanny skill in tracking his quarry, Harry Powell arrives in town. He already knows where John and Pearl are staying and needs only to be reassured that they have a doll with them.

Presenting himself at Miss Cooper's, Powell tries to reclaim his stepchildren. Rachel is suspicious. John hides with the doll under the front porch, where Powell tries to get at him with his switch-blade. The good lady chases the man off her property with a rifle. He returns that night. Miss Cooper wounds him, then stands guard over the barn where he is hiding, until the state police arrive to arrest him for murdering Willa. Released at last from their nightmare, the children can look forward to living in safety in the Cooper home.

Summarized this way, *The Night of the Hunter* does not appear deserving of more success with the critics than it achieved when first released. Meanwhile, its terrifying character and consequent popularity on children's matinée programs seem to call for neither explanation nor comment. Lillian Gish, who played Miss Cooper, has reported that Charles Laughton feared he might have damaged Robert Mitchum's career by casting him, as Harry Powell, in such an evil role.[4] But there are no signs that he made any more effort to compensate for this than to appeal to an élitist audience.

In *The Night of the Hunter* natural locations are mixed with obvious studio sets where exaggerated shadows, underlining the atmosphere of terror, put us in mind of German Expressionism. The critics, however, have shown themselves less than impressed by Laughton's attempt to bring back to cinema some of the qualities he thought film had had in the hands of D. W. Griffith. Are we to take it then that the director of *The Night of the Hunter* alienated almost all except the youngest members of his audience because he devoted himself to communicating his *"vision surréaliste"*? Hardly. There is no evidence to suggest that, at some point in his career, Charles Laughton was converted to Surrealism or that he made his film as a conscious tribute to its underlying principles. There can be no question of supposing he embraced Surrealist ideas or somehow was infused with Surrealist ambitions. If this were indeed the case, his movie might be of less interest than it turns out to be.

The existence of *The Night of the Hunter* proves that Surrealism may make its presence felt in a film where the direct influence of Surrealist theory is not a factor, and as the inadvertent expression of a spirit quite foreign to the environment in which it holds our attention nonetheless. As it stands, Laughton's exploration of the film medium supports the claim put forward by Jacques B. Brunius on the very last page of his *En Marge du cinéma français* (1954): "By reason precisely of the richness of its means, cinema makes it very difficult for one man to have total control over pictures, gestures and words. Very often the film comes from a man's head and from his associates' hands like a ship from a storm, the best way it can, bearing not only what they wanted it to say, but also a few other things that no one was trying to say" (p. 189). This movie does even more. It shows us why Legrand felt entitled to assert, in the Surrealism number of *L'Age du Cinéma* (1951), "First let's understand one another. A film, like a human life, can be Surrealist at some moments. However, it can be wholly so without its author (let's generalize and define him as that two-headed monster, the scriptwriter or storyteller and the director) having set out expressly to make a Surrealist work." Had Charles Laughton shot his movie a few years earlier, we can be confident it would have been cited in the article introduced by Legrand's words, next to *Dark Passage, Laura*, Howard Hawks's *The Big Sleep* (1946), and Joseph H. Lewis's *Gun Crazy* (1949). For it is enriched by features of which the plot summary given above offers no firm indication. These characteristics take on special value for the Surrealist spectator, just as they make it difficult for the critics to know how to handle *The Night of the Hunter*.

As Laughton's film opens, against a dark dreamy background studded with stars, an elderly lady (Miss Cooper, we learn later) is explaining biblical texts to a group of young children whose heads only are visible. Warning against false prophets, she quotes, "Wherefore, by their fruits ye shall know them." These words are still audible as the camera closes in, from above, on an open touring car in which we see a man in dark clothes, paper collar, string tie, and broadbrimmed clerical hat. It is Harry Powell, whose voice we can hear: "Well, now, what's it to be, Lord? Another widow? How many has it been, six?" He glances upward. "Twelve? I disremembered." Touching his hat in salute, he goes on: "You say the word, Lord; I'm on my way . . . You *always* send me money to go forward to preach yore *Word*. A widow with a little wad of bills hid in the sugar bowl. . . . Lord, *I am tired*. Sometimes I wonder if you really understand. Not that you mind the killin's. Yore Book is full o' killin's." We are reminded that we have just seen the first encounter of innocence with Horror in a brief sequence showing the discovery, by some children playing hide-and-go-seek, of a dead woman who possibly may be one of Powell's victims. "But there are a lot of things you *do* hate, Lord," Powell continues, *"perfumed-smelling* things, *lacy* things, things with *curly hair.*"

As an example of Surrealist black humor, these words fully merit a place in André Breton's *Anthologie de l'Humour noir* (first published in 1940), next to the extract from the Marquis de Sade's *Juliette, ou les prospérités du vice* describing a dinner at the home of Count Minsky where the guests help themselves to chunks of roast boy. We have no time, though, to dwell on what Powell has said. Laughton cuts abruptly to a burlesque house. Here Powell occupies an aisle seat, his mouth twisted in anger. Loosely clenched on his thigh, his left hand displays the letters H A T E, that seem to be tatooed on his knuckles. Now he thrusts his fist into his pocket. We hear a click, and a knife blade can be seen sticking through the material of his jacket. Looking upward, away from the stripper on stage, Powell listens, then mutters, "There are too many of *them*. You can't kill the *world*." At this moment a hand drops on his shoulder. A policeman has come to arrest Powell for being in possession of a stolen car.

At the end of his life, Charles Laughton used to like to read from the Bible to children sitting in a circle around him, just as Lillian Gish does in *The Night of the Hunter*. There hardly seems reason to suppose, then, that he made his film in an antireligious spirit. Even so, this movie presents some strange ambiguities that prove to be very appealing to the Surrealist mind. And we cannot dispose of these by arguing that Powell—who proudly insists in court that he is Preacher Harry Powell—is masquerading as a man of God. In James Agee's film-play, he invariably is identified as "PREACHER." Nor does classifying him as a psychotic evangelist explain everything about this movie.

Despite the fact that he is to serve only a thirty-day sentence for car theft, Powell is put in a cell at Moundsville Penitentiary with a convicted murderer, Ben Harper. He hears details of the bank robbery when Harper talks in his sleep. Powell tells his cellmate, "With that ten thousand dollars I could build a Tabernacle make that Wheeling Island Tabernacle look like a chicken-house." Even though he tries to impress upon Harper the benefits of last-minute confession, Ben will not divulge where he hid the money. However, in his sleep, while the preacher listened attentively, he has murmured a clue: "And a little child shall lead them."

When Harper asks what religion he professes, Powell replies, "The religion the Almighty and me worked out betwixt *us*." This personalized religion plainly has its rewards. Preacher Powell still carries his switch-blade, for instance ("I come not with peace, but with a Sword"), and claims, "The Lord blinded mine enemies when they brought me into this evil place." After Harper has fallen asleep, a sock stuffed in his mouth as a safeguard against involuntary confession, Powell picks up his knife, clutching it as he prays, displaying the letters L O V E on the knuckles of his right hand. Who can deny that, as he remarks to God in his prayer, the Almighty knew just what He was doing, when putting Powell "in this very cell at this very time"?—"A man with ten thousand dollars hid somewheres *and* a widder in the makin'."

In Luis Buñuel's movie *Ensayo de un crimen*, released the same year as Laughton's film, Archibaldo de la Cruz offers to cut the throat of a young nun who aspires to the felicities of Heaven. Running off screaming in panic, she accidentally throws herself down an elevator shaft, involuntarily fulfilling her dream without human aid. In the same film-maker's *Susana* (1950), an imprisoned young woman prays to God to work a miracle to release her from captivity. The miracle takes place, and the film's heroine is free to use her sexual talents to disrupt the lives of a respectable bourgeois family. Harry Powell, meanwhile, credits God with engineering the chance he is about to grasp. Whether we interpret events as proof of the intervention of divine will or of some unexplicably beneficent chance operating in defiance of standard morality, the result is the same. John Harper is telling little Pearl a bedtime story—a transposition, obviously, of their own life story—when a menacingly large shadow is cast on their bedroom wall. We recognize Powell's head and shoulders, unmistakable thanks to his broadbrimmed Quaker hat. Outside the house, Powell has paused for a moment near a street lamp before strolling off, singing a hymn we hear for the first time: "Leaning, Leaning. / Leaning on the Everlasting Arms."

Beyond question, Powell is a monster, and as such a figure of terrifying menace to the Harper children. But the standards of moral rectitude are nevertheless ill-defined in *The Night of the Hunter*. After Ben's execution (another widow *made*, this time with the active cooperation of society's law), a prison employee returns to his house on the Moundsville Penitentiary grounds, wearily confessing to his wife that he sometimes feels he should quit his job. She reminds him that what he is doing, these days, is better than being back working in the mine. Apparently, the woman does not know her husband,

Bart, is the prison hangman—she blames his restlessness on Harper's execution which, she says, he did not have to attend. Yet she must have noticed that Bart does not wear a uniform like the other guards. This man who has just left two small children fatherless (Harper, he reports to a uniformed guard, not present at the execution, "carried on some; kicked") goes into the bedroom to tuck his own two children in for the night, carefully freeing one little girl's mouth and throat from the bedding that might impede her breathing. But all's well that ends well. At the close of the film Bart will pronounce it "a privilege" to hang Harry Powell, whose crime and conviction now appear to have renewed his faith and interest in his chosen profession.

Arriving at Cresap's Landing where Willa Harper still lives with her son and daughter, working at Spoon's Ice Cream Parlor, Powell lies about the circumstances under which he knew Ben. John comes in just as Icey Spoon (who believes Willa ought to remarry, so that she can bring up her two children—"The Lord meant that job for two!") is exclaiming, "God works in a mysterious way His wonders to perform." Now the preacher tells John and Pearl "a little story, the tale of Left-Hand-Right-Hand—the tale of Good and Evil," dramatizing love's conquest of hate as his hands grapple, the tatoos visible for all to see. His sermon about love (Mrs. Spoon declares she has never heard the story better told) brings out the fact that the action of *The Night of the Hunter* takes place in an infernal world where adults are incapable of loving.

Even Miss Cooper, who has no time for Powell's little story, is cynical about love, presumably having been deserted by the man who left her with a son from whom she is estranged. She does acknowledge, though, that promiscuity in one of her charges—a thirteen-year-old called Ruby—is an appeal for affection. Uncle Birdie cares about John and Pearl and he would have stood by them gladly, sober. Yet, a longtime widower, the old former river pilot feels his dead wife is spying on him from the photograph in his wharf-boat. Willa shows no real affection for her offspring, and her loyalty to her late husband is short-lived. When Powell lets himself be persuaded to stay on for the Saturday picnic, Mrs. Spoon, in her matchmaking role, exults, "If ever I saw a Sign from Heaven!" Urging Willa to take advantage of the situation, the older woman remarks to some others, "That young lady better look sharp or some smart sister between here and Captina's a-gonna snap him up right from under her nose! She's not the *only* fish in the river!" Icey Spoon, we note, refers to Willa's relationship with Ben in suggestive terms: "That wasn't *love*, that was just *flapdoodle*. . . . When you've been married to a man forty years, you know *that* don't amount to a hill o' beans! I been married to my Walt that long and I swear in all that time I'd just lie there thinking about my canning."

It would be as gross an error tò mistake Mrs. Spoon for a sexually frustrated woman as to believe Surrealists think of love as no more than copulation. Icey Spoon shows where her values lie when commenting, to general agreement, that Willa "is a *fool* to marry for *that*. That's something for a man. The good Lord never meant for a decent woman to want that—not really *want* it! It's all just a fake and a pipe-dream." The inhibitions preventing her from referring openly to sex bring to light an all too familiar attitude to marriage. Much impressed by Karl Marx, Surrealists view this attitude as indicating that, in the bourgeois world, woman demeans herself in entering into a contract, guaranteed by society, whereby she trades her body for security. To them, one of the most revolting aspects of the bourgeois ethic is that it atrophies love.

Willa betrays how deluded she is when she marries Powell out of sexual need no less than to gain security. We are reminded that, entrusting to John the secret of where the stolen money is concealed, Ben Harper ordered his son never to reveal its location to her: "You got common sense. She ain't." We remember, too, that she was incapable of taking seriously the dreadful threat made by the preacher to tear her daughter's arm off. Willa's fate will support the Surrealists' contention that salvation comes from reciprocal love.

Harry Powell is not just incapable of affection. His obsession with a role he considers God-given has rendered him impotent. Crippling him sexually (the judge at his trial is shocked that he, a man of God, was found in a burlesque house), his ambition has exactly the same effect as that of Joseph, the servant in Buñuel's *Le Journal d'une femme de chambre*. The Surrealists are disgusted to see that both these men have lost potency to piety.

Without advance warning ("A husband's one piece of store

good ye never know till you get it home and take the paper
off," Mrs. Spoon observes from experience, supposedly), on
their wedding night Powell says, "You thought, Willa, that the
moment you walked in that door I'd start to paw on you in that
abominable way that men are supposed to do on their wedding night. Ain't that right, now?" He is already in bed and
claims to have been praying when Willa came in, wearing only
nightgown and slippers. He continues, "I think it's time we
made somethin' perfectly clear, Willa. Marriage to me represents the blendin' o' two spirits in the sight of Heaven. . . .
That body was meant for begettin' children. It was *not* meant
for the lust of men. . . . It's the business of this marriage to
mind those two you have now, *not* to beget more." Willa is
crushed and chastened by Powell's exploitation of the
church's traditional guilt inducing argument against sex for
the pleasure of sex. Earlier, when Powell told her the money
was at the bottom of the river, she announced that she felt
clean: "My whole body's a-quivering with cleanness!" Now
she prays earnestly, "Help me to get clean so I can be what
Harry *wants* me to be." Her prayer will be answered: Before
long, Harry will want her dead.

Back home, Willa lies in bed, wearing a prim old woman's
nightgown. Agee's screenplay describes her as "calm and im-
mobile with the ecstasy of a martyr," and as "saint-like." Powell slaps her across the mouth ("Are you through prayin'?")
when she reveals that she at last suspects why he married her.
Meanwhile, guessing that John knows where the money is,
Willa refuses to draw the logical conclusion: "But that ain't the
reason why you married me. I know that much. Because the
Lord just wouldn't let it *be*. He made you marry me so you
could show me the Way and the Life, and the Salvation of my
soul! He did *so*, Harry. So you might say that it was the money
brung us together. The rest of it don't matter." Willa soon is
rewarded for her simple faith in divine providence. While she
is talking, the preacher goes to his jacket to fetch the switch-
blade. Then Willa's new mate stabs her with the knife held in
a fist tatooed L O V E.

The irony of Willa's horrible fate is underscored by the
preacher's inexorable success in wrong-doing. The simple
faith awakened in her by her new evangelist husband (at a
religious meeting of the revivalist kind we hear her "bearing

Courtesy of British National Film Archive/Stills Library

(Top), stylized terror; the rigorous background stylization of German expressionism; (bottom), the killer Harry Powell, with soulful expression, displays his stigmata, outside Miss Cooper's house.

witness" to her sin of driving Harper to robbery and murder)
makes her blind to the danger of her situation. It turns her into
an unresisting victim, in fact. Who can forget her passivity
under the knife? It is as disturbing to watch as Séverine's willing submission to ritual rape, in an early scene of Buñuel's
Belle de jour which we take for sexual fantasy.

Powell's mendacity appears to be unfailingly useful in
furthering his ends. Spreading the story that, possessed by Sa-
tan, Willa has left him, he tells the Spoons that he had an in-
kling of what she would do no later than their wedding night.
Hanging his head, he confides in tortured tones, "She turned
me out of the bed!" Icey Spoon, for whom the marriage bed is
something like the extension of her kitchen table, duly expresses shock but cannot suppress a hint of the thrill of pleasure this news gives her. The preacher goes on, "I *tried* to save
her. . . . But the Devil wins sometimes." He adds, with up-
turned pious eyes, "Can't nobody say *I* didn't do *my* best to
save her." The camera cuts to the river, where fronds bend in
the current. Panning in the direction of the current's flow, it
picks up Willa, seated dead in the submerged car, her hair, as
though alive, tugged by the water. When Walt Spoon expresses tearful admiration for his decision to stay in town to
look after his stepchildren, the preacher responds unctuously,
"Oh, I reckon it was just ordained that way, Brother Spoon."

The simplified explanation that Harry Powell must be a
heartless criminal who just makes use of religion to further his
selfish ends does not hold up. Even if we take them to be
really monologues (the screenplay cautiously states that he
"talks to himself"), his conversations with God testify to some
sense of vocation. Hence it is difficult indeed to draw a line
between cynicism and genuine conviction, as we listen to
what he says. When he loses his temper, reducing little Pearl
to tears and so inducing John to tell where the money is hidden, Powell remarks, "Well, I declare! Sometimes I think poor
old John might make it to Heaven yet!" Down in the cellar a
few moments later, he finds the boy has lied. Powell seizes the
lad and—his sincerity beyond doubt, the screenplay emphasizes—cries, "The Lord's a-talkin' to me now! He's a-sayin', 'A
liar is an abomination before mine eyes!' " Producing his
trusty switch-blade, he presses it to John's neck, threatening,
"Speak, or I'll cut your throat and leave you to drip like a hog

hung up in butcherin' time." The prospect is so terrifying to Pearl ("You can save him, little bird") that she lets out the truth about the doll.

Applied behind a façade of Christian charity, Harry Powell's terror tactics have succeeded. It is no surprise to find that, when Miss Cooper is skeptical about his ability to raise the children without a wife, he has his answer pat: "The Lord will provide." With a glance at the doll Pearl dropped in her eagerness to hug her "Daddy Powell," upon his arrival outside the Cooper home, he exclaims soulfully, "The Lord is merciful. Oh what a day *this* is!"

Only Rachel Cooper seems able to sense ulterior motives in the preacher's conduct. In the end, Powell's Nemesis turns out to be an unsentimental woman, capable of loving children, whom Agee identifies without irony as "our heroine at last," the moment she first appears.[5] How much store, though, can one set by the happy outcome with which *The Night of the Hunter* ends, given the circumstances that bring it about?

When Rachel Cooper prepares to read from the Scriptures, John walks out of the house. He makes it very clear indeed that he has had enough of Bible-spouters. Meanwhile, the evidence against the likelihood that right will triumph over wrong brings us close to inferring one thing, if nothing else. Perhaps Charles Laughton does not share Harry Powell's belief that the Almighty condones murder. All the same, in his filming of James Agee's screenplay he displays a skepticism that may give truly religious persons cause for concern. It may not be the case that one has to be a child to escape reservations about the happy ending in *The Night of the Hunter*. Even so, the way love wins out over hate, in conformity with Agee's film-play, raises more questions than it answers.

While Miss Cooper is belligerently running Powell off her property, he is ranting, "The Lord God *Jehovah* will guide my hand in vengeance. You devils! You whores of Babylon!" By the time the movie is over, however, it looks as though he was deluded after all. It seems that God, whose Book warns against false prophets—ravening wolves in sheep's clothing—is not mocked. "Lord, save little children"—Rachel Cooper's prayer has the force of incontrovertible truth. For, according to her simple philosophy, John and Pearl are sure to "abide," to "endure," like all children. But what gives them the chance to do

so by fortuitously disposing of Harry Powell, murderer of four-
teen adults?

Has God deserted Powell? Or has the man's luck simply run
out? If Miss Cooper is to be considered the instrument of divine retribution, then we have to admit that she comes neither
in peace nor with a sword, as the preacher does. She carries a
pump-gun, knows how to use it, and does not hesitate to do so.
Her weapon at the ready, she looks remarkably like the nun
seen loading her rifle (presumably during the time of unrest in
the Belgian Congo where, as so often, the missionary spirit
and colonialism went hand in hand), in a photograph on the
cover of the first issue of the magazine *BIEF: action surréaliste*, that appeared three years after *The Night of the
Hunter* was released.

Making good his threat to return after dark, Harry Powell
signals his presence outside the Cooper home, as he did outside Harpers', by singing the hymn he seems to prefer. Rachel
sits on guard before a window, her gun across her knees. Now
a curious thing happens. She joins in singing words that have
come to have cruelly ironical value in this film. Referring to
Agee's text for some kind of explanation, we find it weakly
indecisive. We learn that the woman sings either to comfort
herself or (more improbably) to drown out the preacher's
voice, which easily dominated the hymn singing interlude at
the Cresap's Landing picnic.

There is no indication in Agee's film-play that the version of
the hymn Rachel will sing is to differ in any way from Powell's, with which we are quite familiar by now. Nevertheless
the preacher, devoted to the vengeful Old Testament Jehovah,
sings as usual, "Leaning, leaning, ..." Meanwhile Miss
Cooper invokes the New Testament Jesus who, out of love,
sacrificed Himself for mankind: "Lean on Jesus, lean on
Jesus, / Safe and secure from all alarms." There is no way of
telling whether this interesting revealing variation was introduced by Charles Laughton on his own initiative, after discussion with his scriptwriter, or at someone else's suggestion. Its
origin makes no difference to the outcome, anyway. The effect
is one that nobody seems to have foreseen. This brief episode
offers the audience a harmonized duet, inexplicably implying
common accord between Rachel and Powell, rather than pre-

senting the equivalent of rousing parliamentary cheers and counter-cheers.

Miss Cooper is distracted momentarily when Ruby, whose interest in the opposite sex holds no secrets for her ("You were looking for love, Ruby, in the only foolish way you knowed how. We *all* need love, Ruby"). Looking out again through her window, Rachel discovers that the preacher is no longer in sight. As an owl swoops down at a baby rabbit and its victim's stricken cry is heard, Miss Cooper, still clutching her gun, comments, "It's a hard world for little things."

It can go hard for the rest of us too, she demonstrates. Obviously blessed with excellent reflexes, when Powell appears inside the house and stumbles over the cat, she shoots him in the shoulder, on the L O V E side (not on the left side, as foreseen in the film-play). Rachel makes no further mention of Jesus and no allusion to all-forgiving love. She has shown that love is well and good in its place, but that dispensing Christian charity indiscriminately would be foolhardy. Surrealists can only view with amusement flagrant signs of the inner contradictions of religious teaching in this woman who, while yet loving according to biblical injunction, still comes close to violating one of the Ten Commandments, and then makes a businesslike phone call: "Get your state troopers out to my place. I got somethin' trapped in my barn."

With an exactitude of detail prescribed by James Agee's film-play, Harry Powell's arrest reproduces the circumstances of Ben Harper's. Like Harper, Powell is knocked to the ground by efficiently brutal state troopers. After uttering the anguished cry, "No! No!" John throws himself on the prostrate man. He pleads with his father to take back the money, as it spills out of the doll with which he beats his stepfather. Whether or not we find plausible the effects of physical and mental strain in this young boy, it is evident that we are meant to elucidate his behavior in light of formal parallelism. At this moment, then, cinematic technique serves to guide our interpretation. No such guidance, though, shows us how we may reconcile the fundamental ethical contradictions that mark *The Night of the Hunter*, turning it into something more than a horror story. Charles Laughton closes his movie with Miss Cooper giving John (who has always coveted one) a watch as a

Christmas present. His film ends during the season of good will to all men, with a mob (Mr. and Mrs. Spoon prominently in sight) bent on lynching Preacher Harry Powell, whose life the police carefully preserve so that it can be taken by Hangman Bart, whose front door—by which stands a child's perambulator—displays a Christmas wreath.

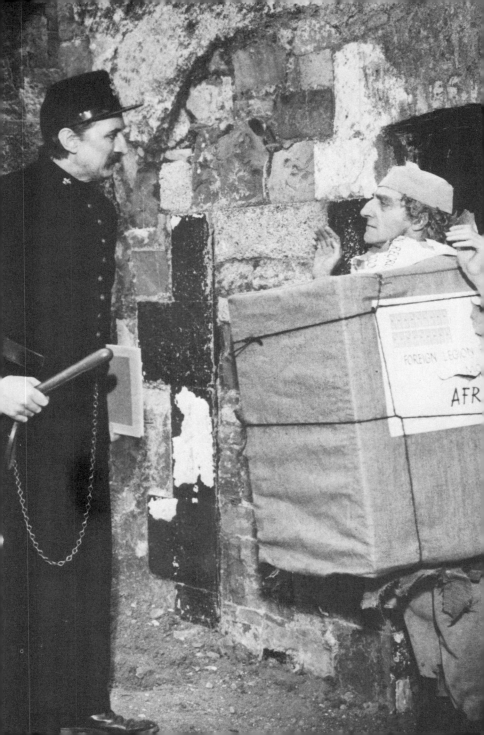

8

Marty Feldman:
The Last Remake of Beau Geste
(1977)

REVIEW of the history of cinema during its earliest years lets us observe film concurrently exploring two divergent directions. The tendency to use the movies as an instrument for recording external reality with unprecedented accuracy (whether it be by showing a baby at breakfast or a train entering a station) is counterbalanced from the first by a new tradition, offering comedy of a kind that expands the bounds of lived experience.

In a *Dictionnaire abrégé du surréalisme* published for the first time in 1938, on the occasion of an International Surrealist Exhibition in Paris, Salvador Dalí is quoted as saying, "What can be expected of surrealism and what could be expected of a certain so-called *comic* cinema is all that deserves to be considered." Nevertheless—and this is something that Surrealists see as a disappointingly limiting effect of the introduction of sound into cinema—the realist tradition was the one that came to command most respect in Hollywood, as elsewhere. Violation of its assumptions and usages fell subject to restriction. If not for excuse, then henceforth departing from the conventions of realism called at least for some kind of apologetic justification.

The net result achieved by the beginning of the nineteen-forties may be assessed if we take a moment to consider Edward Cline's *Never Give a Sucker an Even Break* (1941), based on a story by one Otis Criblecoblis—none other than the film's star, W. C. Fields.

The action of this movie that Ado Kyrou (ignoring Cline) treats as Fields's masterpiece is set on the lot of a motion picture company. Here we see W. C. Fields playing the very Fields characters that his previous movies have rendered

In a letter dated January 19. 1979, Marty Feldman comments that the photo of Digby in the package "seems to me a perfect illustration of a point—the point being that as writer-director-actor, I am a package. Although the sequence was not used in the picture, it seems to reinforce, if obliquely, the Magritte quotation." (See discussion in the preface)

familiar to audiences. As Surrealists are not slow to notice, under his own name he appears now as a man at odds with the Hollywood environment. They would say that, at Esoteric Pictures, he displays true health in a sick world of conventionality and submissive acceptance.

The film is hardly under way when Fields visits the office of Mr. Pangborn (played by Franklin Pangborn) for a story conference. Preparing to read the script he has written, he murmurs, "Of course, this is only a rough draft. You'll have to bear with me half a tick." How, though, could Pangborn consent to bear with a man who announces that Mrs. Pangborn will be required to wear a beard for the circus scene and will have to go to a barber shop to get a shave? And what about the prescribed "long-shot of streamlined plane with open-air rear observation compartment"? The studio executive's reaction is as violent as it is foreseeable: "Just a moment, Mr. Fields. There's a limit to everything! This script is an insult to a man's intelligence, even mine! You drop from an airplane 10,000 feet in the air and you land on a divan without a scratch. You play Post Office with a beautiful blonde and then you throw yourself over a cliff in a basket. It's impossible, inconceivable, incomprehensible. And besides that—it's no good. And as for the continuity, it's—it's terrible."

Meanwhile, the film has cut away from the conference room to enact scenes described by Fields, including his fall from the open-air observation compartment in pursuit of his whisky flask ("Drown in a vat of whisky, eh?" runs one of his memorable utterances, "Death where is thy sting?"). *Never Give a Sucker an Even Break* succeeds as outrageous comedy because, writing and acting in it, W. C. Fields enjoys the best of both worlds. He is free to indulge in fantasy of the kind that the setting of his most recent film, *The Bank Dick*, ruled out. At the same time, letting Pangborn criticize everything rationally and logically unacceptable in the script submitted by Fields, Cline has paid lip service to Hollywood's conception of viable cinema, while yet putting together a movie that departs from and denies that conception. This is one of the most striking features of the movie. It claims and takes advantage of total liberty of expression, even as it makes a gesture of acceptance in the direction of regulatory controls usually unquestioned in Hollywood. To the Surrealist, Cline's film thus stands out as a significant demonstration of subversive intent concealed beneath conformity and reclaiming cinema from platitudinous conventional realism.

Whether or not we can agree that the Surrealists are right in supposing subversion to have been the predetermined goal in *Never Give a Sucker an Even Break*, it is not hard to see one important thing. To the Surrealists' complete satisfaction, this W. C. Fields vehicle bears out their long-established theory that, in Hollywood, Surrealism can make headway only where the ground rules of commercialism are circumvented somehow or other. If this film has a special message for the Surrealist, therefore, it seems to be that some expedient is required to break the framework of Hollywood cinema production, or at least to crack it sufficiently to let in comic elements habitually excluded.

Turning to Marty Feldman's version of a Hollywood classic, we encounter clear signs that the ground rules in Hollywood have changed significantly over the period of almost four decades since Cline and Fields worked together. As a consequence—and as a result, too, of a perceptible change in the moviegoing public's mood—the director of *The Last Remake of Beau Geste* (1977) needs to resort to no subterfuge and to very little compromise indeed, in order to be able to bring before his audience a kind of comedy that, in Cline's day, surely would have failed for lack of financial backing; supposing, that is, some scriptwriter had been bold enough to conceive its presentation on film worth attempting and had managed to find a producer to share his views.

The title Feldman chose for a film derived from William A. Wellman's 1939 movie is an ironic reminder of the sad history of cinema remakes in Hollywood. With quite disheartening regularity, film-makers bent on turning past successes to account in the box office have demonstrated that reworking a movie (*King Kong*, for example) seems fated to be a disastrous enterprise. It appears that not one remake can stand comparison with the original on which it is based. [Editor's note: This is true even of Wellman's 1939 version of *Beau Geste* (the object of Feldman's satire), which is a remake of Herbert Brenon's 1926 silent classic. Ronald Colman starred as the doomed Beau Geste in that version of P. C. Wren's novel, which has also become the classic stereotype of the romance of the French Foreign Legion in the Sahara, burlesqued by Laurel and Hardy in *Beau Hunks* (1931).] And yet, coauthor of the script as well as director, Marty Feldman succeeds where others have failed. He does so because the irreverent spirit in which he approaches the material to be adapted leads him to something other than mere exploitation of the time-honored sort.

Feldman does not aim to copy the film on which he models his own. Instead, he takes for granted his audience's acquaintance with Wellman's movie or, alternatively, with the P. C. Wren novel Wellman brought to the screen (or again with Wren's *Beau Sabreur* — it really makes no difference). What matters is that he proceeds at once to decry the values that gave purpose and meaning to the action of *Beau Geste*, sustained it, and made it impressive: a veritable *beau geste*, in fact. Doing so, he offers the public a film that accords perfectly with the Surrealist ethic.

Without sketching exaggerated claims for the supposed expansion of Surrealism's influence in Hollywood, one can observe that the existence of Feldman's lavishly produced film lends support to André Breton's declaration that Surrealism "is what will be." Of course, there is nothing very mysterious here. By the time the United States' involvement in Vietnam was at an end, the thinking element of the American public no longer could avoid certain questions and, in increasing numbers, making deductions some of which the Surrealists in France had reached years before — largely in reaction to French colonial policy in North Africa and Indochina. Moreover, *The Last Remake of Beau Geste* is the work of an Englishman, member of a race that had to accept the collapse of its empire some time before the United States ever began trying to implement an imperialist policy of its own. Voicing some of the conclusions that, by the mid-nineteen-seventies, had become obvious, and pursuing their implications within the framework of film comedy, Feldman could expect to find an indulgent audience, if not a fully approving one. As little as ten years earlier, we can be sure, he would have encountered measurable hostility such as, for instance, had greeted Robert Aldrich's movie *Attack* in 1956, before the advent of something that many Americans declined to acknowledge to be a war and preferred to call the Korean Conflict.

Just enough survives from Wellman's production to legitimize the designation "remake" for the screenplay on which Feldman collaborated with Chris Allen after coauthoring the original story. Beau Geste steals the family heirloom, the Blue Water, a sapphire compared to which, his father declares with pride, some of the world's most famous diamonds are "pieces of shit." To escape punishment for his crime, Beau enlists in the French Foreign Legion. Taking the blame for the theft to protect his brother and the family name, Digby Geste goes to jail, then escapes and soon joins Beau in North Africa. Even before the plot has progressed this far, however, it is evident that remaking *Beau Geste* has not meant simply replacing a black-and-white movie with a magnificent color one, filmed in Panavision. *Beau Geste* has been transformed from top to bottom. Inherited plot is just one of a number of features handled with disruptive irony and corrosive humor.

Even before the action begins the mood is set, in this Universal picture. We see Feldman destroying the revolving globe that is Universal Pictures' trademark. Then, in mock documentary reportage style, he announces, voice over, "The place: North Africa. The year: 1906. Our story starts right —here." His finger jabs a map of the Sahara Desert. Immediately a line of marching legionnaires look up at a receding larger-than-life digit, several of them falling into a big hole it has left in the sand. Disproportion is already a key to absurdity.

Now, by means of a superimposed title we are informed that the story really started some years earlier. The picture of a desert fort is replaced by that of Geste Manor. Here Sir Hector Geste is awaiting the birth of his first son, whom he intends to call Beau and for whom he sings a song of joyous anticipation: "My boy Beau / Will be tall and as strong as a tree. / I know!" Hearing a child's first cry, he yells, "Cowardly little swine! Is *that* what he thinks a hero's like, bawling like a sissy? I'll beat some courage into him. . . . Out of my way, Dr. Crippen. I want to discipline my son." Breeding *will* have its way. Geste is about to start his offspring on the road to corporal punishment which the English Public School system associates with character building and, coincidentally, gives the French cause to speak of flagellation as *le vice anglais*.

From its opening moments, *The Last Remake* appears to advance idiosyncratically. It is, however, rich in allusions—some of them obscure enough to qualify as semiprivate jokes—that give it texture. A parody of Billy Bigelow's song "My boy Bill," prompted by parallel circumstance in Rodgers and Hammerstein's musical *Carousel*, "My boy Beau" is shouted raucously by an actor, Trevor Howard, hero of numerous British stiff-upper-lip patriotic war films (gone, but not forgotten. . .). Howard finds himself playing, here, a role that ridicules the kind of part to which his professional reputation owes so much.

It is Sir Hector's misfortune that the family physician is the infamous Dr. Crippen, who manages to dispose of yet another wife (this time, someone else's) while delivering her of a daughter. "I have no requirements for a daughter," shouts the grand old soldier for whom it is "wonderful news" that England "has been plunged headlong into a bloody and disastrous war" against the French in the Sudan: "The piles of rotting corpses, the stench of blood! How it titillates these jaded nostrils. I suppose I'm just an old-fashioned sentimentalist," muses this country gentleman who probably thinks of fox hunting as a sport.

Sir Hector's antiquated butler, Crumble (one of whose tasks is to walk his master's stuffed British bulldog in the grounds of Geste Manor, where it dutifully cocks a leg, miraculously grown back after being lost in the Sudan campaign), is played by Spike Milligan, son of a professional soldier in the Indian Army (read: British Army of Occupation). Milligan is an entertainer who never neglected an opportunity to poke fun at the military in the scripts of his decade-long radio series, *The Goon Show*, which attracted favorable attention from the Surrealists.[1] The treacherous Foreign Legion general who sells guns to the enemy is played by Henry Gibson, best known to American audiences as the effeminate poet of television's *Laugh In*. His name is Pecheur (*pécheur*, sinner, or perhaps *pêcheur*, fisherman). His aide-de-camp's name is less ambiguous, pointing directly to the quickest route to promotion in any military organization. It is Merdmanger (*merde-manger*, eat shit). Cpl. Boldini of the Legion is Roy Kinnear, who engag-

ingly narrated the story of the activities of African nationalist,
Dr. Banda, as "Little Black Banda," in one of the most biting
skits offered by the BBC's vitriolic *This Is The Week That Was*.
Assuming the role of handsome Beau Geste, Michael York dis-
sociates himself from the naive romanticizing of war that
seemed to make him perfect for his role in *The Three Mus-
keteers*, directed by Richard Lester, long-time producer of *The
Goon Show*. Only the film's "special guest star," Gary Cooper—seen in the part of Beau, as he played it in 1939—remains a
prisoner to the ethic of the past.

James Earl Jones as the Sheikh is, meanwhile, the Black
man's answer to a Great White Hope: the Lone Ranger. At the
moment of defeat, he shouts "Abdul away!" as his horse rears
like Silver. When, later, his Bedouin tribesmen attack their
fort, the legionnaires' bugler first sounds "Post Time" and
then, as for the benefit of a crowd at a football game,
"Charge."

Feldman's movie is characterized by frequent visual and
auditory reminiscences that serve to relocate elements just as
in Surrealist pictorial *collage*. The blackout scene during
which the Blue Water disappears is familiar to anyone who
knows the Marx Brothers' *Love Happy*. Sgt. Markov, the Legion NCO, is struck down by a Black soldier wearing a hook in
place of his right hand—an unmistakable reversal of the climax
of *A Man is Ten Feet Tall*. When Markov rides away for good,
dragging Boldini behind him in a horse trough, we hear the
music that regularly closes Warner Bros. "Looney Tune" car-
toon films. And at the end of *The Last Remake* it looks for a
moment as though Beau and his stepmother are going to die of
thirst in the desert, in a scene like the one that brings
Clouzot's *Manon* (screenplay by Jean Ferry) to its conclusion.

The pattern is too regular to allow us to speak of mere coincidence. It is especially worth noting, therefore, that when we
first see the dread sergeant, one of whose aphorisms runs,
"Life is as brief as a butterfly's fart, but death is something
you'll have forever," the camera pauses long enough for us to
read, tatooed on the back of one hand, the word "Hate." On
the other, the visible letters "Lo" introduce not "Love" (as in
The Night of the Hunter) but "Loathing." Retrospectively,
Markov's explanation—reminding us how many war criminals

are said to have found refuge in the French Foreign Legion after 1945 — enlightens Harry Powell's psychological state as well as his own: "Some may consider that I am excessively cruel. But there's a *reason* for this cruelty: I *enjoy* it."

Allusions of some kinds are benign, in *The Last Remake of Beau Geste*. During a commercial break interrupting the desert battle scene, Honest Hakkim is seen selling used camels: "Shalom, salaam, welcome, effendis. I want to tell you somethin'. You want a good set of humps? Come to Camel Lot." At the other extreme, though, Feldman is willing to release more disturbing associations. Beau and Digby plant the French flag in desert sand, evoking an incident that inspired the U. S. Marine Corps' monument to its dead. And, denied a son, Hector Geste goes looking for one in a quite Dickensian orphanage (we see a boy cuffed with a Bible and called "wicious little varmint" when caught reading it) named Wormwood and Gall, after London's prison for men, Wormwood Scrubs. During a fist fight, one boy immediately captures his attention by the ability to floor his opponents with blows not all of which would meet with the Marquis of Queensbury's approval. "That's him! That's Beau!" the old man cries in excitement. Meanwhile the boy, Obediah Spittle, is bathed in unearthly light, like Holman Hunt's Christ — complete with halo. Like Saul of Tarsus, Obediah will take a new name and, "naturally," promises Sir Hector, "he will be brought up with an English gentleman's attitude and love of slaughter."

Because Miss Wormwood (who has sold her own offspring) refuses to "split the pair," Sir Hector is obliged to adopt, together with Obediah, his identical twin, Digby, who will not benefit from receiving a new name. From the first, Obediah-Beau is blessed with a refined accent of impeccable purity. Prepubescent Digby, however, is cursed with an Ulster brogue (in part, this film was shot in Ireland). With maturity, it inexplicably yields to Feldman's own unmistakably stigmatizing London tone. "Somehow," Feldman comments philosophically, in the role of Digby, "Beau was much more identical than me." Thus Beau grows up to inherit the prejudices of his adoptive class. On a postcard sent his brother from the Sahara, he reports that Markov (played by Peter Ustinov), "the chap in charge," is "O. K. for a Kraut, but — *not* one of us!"

Beau's place at table in the legionnaires' mess hall has a

Two Ages of Man.   *Credit: Universal Studio*

reserved sign, prominently displayed. His table during the dance (to music by Legionnaire von Braun and his Band of Renaun) is discreetly decorated with a little Union Jack. Yet he is too intelligent to do more than go through the motions of living up to his station in life. It is left to Digby to accept the burden of being an honorable English gentleman. Brought to trial before a judge (impersonated by a Welshman, Hugh Griffith), he is given a taste of British justice, which reserves a more severe penalty for cruelty to animals than for child battering. At the close of a farcical scene resembling an auction, in which his sentence is pushed higher and higher by bids from the gallery as well as from the court, Digby ends up with "nine hundred and fifty-six years or life, whichever is the longer." So the American penal system is not forgotten, either. Transported by a sense of righteousness, Digby intones piously, "Then I have done whatever it is that I have done for Beau and for the sacred name of Geste." While he is speaking, the camera lens closes and threatens to blacken the whole screen before he can finish his peroration. As Lady Flavia puts it succinctly, "Screw the name of Geste!" Central to the family coat of arms, we are reminded, is the rear view of a horse. When, at the end of the movie, Digby suggests that all they have to do, now, is take the Blue Water back to their father, Beau echoes their stepmother's views: "Screw Sir Hector!" The venerable military hero, who has been "alive and dying" ever since Beau left for Africa, succumbs with a roar and his daughter, Isabel, turns his bulldog on its back pushing its protruding tongue back into its mouth.

Sir Hector's slow passing keeps in sight two themes, vulgarity and sex, closely interwoven in Feldman's movie. Returning from a successful campaign in the Sudan wishing he was only seventy-five again, the old warrier has brought with him a ravishing young wife, Flavia, who is determined to redecorate Geste Manor: "I thought we might do something bizarre with a chandelier and some ostrich feathers." Betraying his erotic obsession, in his reply that he hopes he has the energy, Sir Hector illustrates the principles of Surrealist dialogue, as described in Breton's first manifesto. He hurries upstairs to wait for Flavia in the conjugal bedroom and calls down, a few moments later, "Hurry up! I can't hang on this chandelier much longer!" Soon afterward an anguished cry is heard. In due course, Dr. Crippen reports that Sir Hector "over-came himself." Has Trevor Howard (who failed to copulate with his illicit partner in Lean's chaste treatment of adultery, *Brief Encounter*) learned a lesson for which Sir Hector pays a high price? "This," remarks Crippen with utmost gravity, "may be the first recorded case of death by ecstasy." Later, in the governor's bed, at the jail where Digby has begun serving his mammoth sentence, the following dialogue takes place under a blanket embroidered "H. M. Prisons":

GOVERNOR: "Delighted you came, my dear. And I'd like you to know that you made a happy man feel very–old. Now let's get this straight. In exchange for an hour of amorous dalliance . . ."

FLAVIA: "Just under four minutes, actually."

GOVERNOR: "Really? Well one does what one can. You wish me to contrive an escape from my *own* prison?"

FLAVIA: "Precisely. . . . It's been a business doing pleasure with you."

GOVERNOR: "Oh, how power corrupts! Thank God!"

On the door of the cell (packed with enough prisoners to remind any redblooded Englishman of the Black Hole of Calcutta) where Digby is in solitary confinement—"crowded gaol conditions, you know," apologizes the governor—are chalked the unedifying words, "Queen Victoria is a dyke": possible news to the Prince Consort by whom she had numerous children. In the orphanage, behind a statue (hand raised in pontifical blessing) can be read the admonishment, "Give up yourselves to the ways of the Lord." During a violent squabble among the inmates, the statue loses all except two raised fingers. Then a single digit survives to replace a British rude gesture with an American one. Meanwhile, general destruction has reduced the lapidary phrase to "up yours."

At Fort Zindeneuf, Boldini slips into the communal shower where Beau is singing manfully in a voice not his own, dubbed with scant regard for the niceties of postsynchronization. The corporal institutes a determined search for the Blue Water that causes the handsome young man to shriek. "Sorry," mutters Boldini, visibly embarrassed. "I was looking for the soap." A sound like that of a cork withdrawn from a bottle is audible, just like that heard when Feldman withdrew his finger from the Sahara sand and when one of the Sheikh's tribesmen pulled from under his mount's tail the nozzle of an Ajax Camel Inflator, inserted after the dromedary's hump had been punctured by a bullet. As Boldini sidles away, Beau gives a slow, knowing nod. It is apparent that, like T. E. Lawrence—though less indulgently—he has learned to live with homosexuality in the Arabian Desert.

One might dismiss details of this sort as evidence of an adolescent mentality, marring *The Last Remake of Beau Geste*. To the Surrealist, though, they fall into place when viewed in light of his preference for bad taste, vigorously defended against bourgeois good taste by Dalí among other Surrealists. Moreover, he finds them to be noteworthy elements in a film where sex serves as a counterforce, opposed to moral and ethical standards quite repugnant to him. Certainly, they have to be acknowledged as contributing actively to severing confining family ties and to ridiculing an institution he holds in contempt: the army.

Between March of 1831 when the French Foreign Legion

was founded and October 1962 when it quit North Africa, it lost more than nine hundred officers, in excess of three thousand noncommissioned officers, and ten times as many legionnaires, representing no less than forty nationalities.[2] The Legion can pride itself on having been the most decorated French unit of the 1914-18 war. This is a sad distinction, in the eyes of a Surrealist, to whom the Legion tradition of parading Capt. Jean Danjou's wooden hand before the First Regiment every Camerone Day (April 30) must appear less inspiring than ghoulish. At first, therefore, he can look only with suspicion upon the hero of *The Last Remake*, standing in line with other new recruits at the Legion depot. These men who have responded to the glamor of the Foreign Legion include a Mexican (complete with guitar), a kilted Scotsman (with bagpipes but no visible haggis), a matador (in *traje de luces*), a bearded black-garbed individual with doctor's bag (a human foot, wearing a sock, protruding from it), inscribed Jack T. Ripper, a thug in nun's habit, Dostoievski, and a blind man (officer material, according to Markov). At the end of the line, impeccably turned out in English gentleman's casual attire, complete with boater, stands Beau Geste. "I am a soldier, sergeant. I trust I shall prove a loyal and a brave one!"

Beau is not incorrigibly heroic, however. After Markov has been struck down with a blow from the Black legionnaire's hook for invoking "Fatherland und Kaiser," Beau responds to the stirring cry, "We're behind you, sir. We'll die to the last man if you say so!" with glad tidings: "No! You can be free." The legionnaires la-la *John Brown's Body* as he continues, "For your own sakes, desert! Get out of here. Go and be rotten to people. But—do it for a decent living wage!" When all its defenders have abandoned Fort Zindeneuf, he expounds his new philosophy: "Heroism? Medals? Medals are like hemorrhoids, Digby. In the end every arsehole gets them." Beau now uses the picture of a Viking funeral he has carried with him for so long (as a reminder of the way he would like to depart this life) to start a fire under his uniform before deserting. The ashes he leaves behind will be taken for his mortal remains. So, because "The Legion always honors its 'eroes," Gen. Pecheur will flush them ceremoniously down a toilet ringed with black bow ties.

Whereas Beau escapes being depraved by his environment,

Markov cannot. Gen. Pecheur describes him as "vicious, cruel, sadistic," in short, "a soldier to the skin." Markov, whose sergeant's stripes are, indeed, tatooed on his arms, owns an assortment of stick-on scars, some of which look authentically Prussian. He keeps them in a metal box labeled, according to the inverted syntax of British Army quartermasters, "Scars various." His medals, though, he wears at all times, looking like one of the Surrealist painter Baj's grotesque generals, bespattered with military decorations. The farcically monstrous sergeant lives by the code of Gen. François de Negrier, who holds a place in the lore of the French Foreign Legion since he greeted a volunteer battalion arriving in Indochina in 1883 with the words, "You legionnaires are soldiers in order to die, and I am sending you where you can die." Negrier appears to have set the standard, where Markov is concerned. For the latter comments, "Those who survived did quite vell. Those who got killed did rather *better!*"

Because he is an incurable military man, Markov is the object of relentless mockery that Surrealists heartily approve. Most of the time he wears a metal pegleg, just like his horse and the uniformed teddy bear that is his fetish, the way the bulldog is Sir Hector's. For war he draws upon his wide selection of artificial legs, selecting his battle leg (adorned with a mailed fist that embraces his calf) or one that is a genuine Surrealist object: a "veepon" that can be aimed and fired like a small cannon. The general and Lady Flavia arrive at his quarters the very moment Boldini is helping him prepare for bed by detaching his artificial leg. The latter needs to be replaced by a dress leg, before the visitors can be admitted. From outside the door, they hear Markov cry out, "Keep screwing, Boldini. Faster, Boldini, faster. Can't you screw any faster than that? Every thousand miles this thing must be oiled.—Oh, I'm coming, general. I'm coming!" Pecheur is embarrassed; Flavia, amused.

Later, Markov harangues the troops: "Ve march at first light. Our moment of reckoning vill come at Fort Zindeneuf. All day yesterday the Sheikh's men have been attacking the fort. Many brave legionnaires have been killed in a futile effort to defend it. Tomorrow, you vill be killed doing something equally futile. You're only privileged to die vonce. Don't schrew it up!" As the legionnaires march out under the brave motto, "Fort Zindeneuf or bust!!" from a balcony above the parade ground Gen. Pecheur salutes them: "Adieu, adieu mes braves, mes petits soldats! May God go with you. *I* have *better* things to do." He turns away from the window and struts, naked from the tunic down, to the bed where Lady Flavia is waiting for him to resume working his way through the *Kama Sutra by Numbers (Legion Issue).*

As the prison governor finds out, in *The Last Remake* the confrontation of duty and desire, of obligation and pleasure that, to a Surrealist, can lead to only one acceptable resolution is centered on the person of Hector's new wife. Intent on regaining possession of the Blue Water, Flavia contrives Digby's escape so as to be able to follow him by hansom cab to wherever Beau can be. In the desert, the liberative process enabling Beau to escape the trap of military glory frees him, also, from respect for social and moral taboos that Surrealists abhor. One night, he demonstrates most satisfactorily what lies behind the old musical favorite, "I want a girl / Just like the girl / That married dear old Dad":

FLAVIA: "Did the earth move for you, darling?"
BEAU: "I did feel *something.*—I only hope I lived up to what a mother should expect from her son."

From childhood up, Beau has been unencumbered with feelings, leaving it to Digby to experience them for him. So "feeling *something*" with Lady Flavia, whom thereafter he continues to call "Mother," is a tribute indeed to the joys of intercourse with her. It will bring him, very soon, to reject his duty as a soldier, to desert, and to go off with his stepmother. When Digby protests, "I won't let you not be a hero," Beau knocks him out. It is Digby then who will be decorated as Fort Zindeneuf's last surviving defender—with a medal for cooking chocolate mousse, as it turns out.

Does this mean that, still bearing a stigma he shares with his adoptive sister Isabel (who "practiced and practiced, and became an accomplished—virgin"), Digby is beyond redemption? It seems this is the case, when we see him stood up before a firing squad for refusing to explain the mystery of the abandoned fort: "A Geste *never* talks!" Within a tight semicircle of rifle muzzles, he declaims, "I'm prepared to die so that Beau's name may live. Would you expect me to betray my brother, my country, my Isabel, my honour?" The order to aim is given. " 'Silence unto death' is the family motto. Shall I talk now? Ha! You expect me to talk when all I could preserve is my own measly worthless life? [*ironic laugh*] You're bloody right, I'll talk! I'll talk! I'll talk! Just try and stop me! I'll talk! I'll talk!"

Good sense having led Digby to set aside values a Surrealist deems false, he is reunited with Isabel and enacts a ludicrous reunion scene with her:

DIGBY: "Don't speak! Just let me look at you for a moment. And then *I* won't speak and then you can look at *me* for a moment." [*pause*]
ISABEL: "Enough?"
DIGBY: "Enough!—Isabel, you know I've always felt . . ."
ISABEL: "I know. But you know that Beau and I . . ."
DIGBY: "I know. But did you know that *he* and I . . . ?"
ISABEL: "I know. And you know that if we didn't know . . ."
DIGBY: "I know. You know I know."
ISABEL: "Yes! I know."
DIGBY: "How little we know."
ISABEL: "I know."
DIGBY: "Then you know that Beau is . . ."
ISABEL: "No! Beau is what?"
DIGBY: "Beau is—not!"

Beneath this gibberish we find clarification of the relationship binding hero-worshipping Digby to Beau and both of them to Isabel. Now, lying in Isabel's arms while, sustained by champagne on a distant sundrenched beach, Beau rests in Flavia's embrace. Digby finally has tangible proof that his twin is still alive. Recalling that he always used to know what Beau was feeling, he glances demurely down at his own body. In this postromantic age, an erection—a humanizing indication of sexual potency that some will call vulgar—links the brothers across thousands of miles.

So far as plot goes, *The Last Remake of Beau Geste* explodes illusions: Markov rides away thinking he has the Blue Water, not a false precious stone; glory and family name are tattered myths by the time we hear the song—burlesquing the sentimental favorite from *Man of La Mancha*—that accompanies the final credits.[3] The end of the movie, in short, confirms what we have heard and seen along the way.

Muttering, "I think I've discovered another movie cliché," Crumble totters around a whirling newspaper carrying banner headlines that announce the end of fighting in the Sudan. With the legionnaires gone from Fort Zindeneuf, Beau confronts Markov and another film cliché is ridiculed:

BEAU: "So! The obligatory duel to the death!"
MARKOV: "Of course.—As hero and villain, it is *expected* of us. . . . Do you desire to duel *with* or *without* conversation?"
BEAU: "*With*, I think. Yes, definitely *with*."

By their own admission (made directly to the camera), the ensuing dialogue is less than comprehensible to the duelists.

Similarly, after a skirmish in the desert, Digby's naive remark, "Looks like we've beaten them off, Beau" draws from his knowledgeable brother the sage response, "They'll be back at dawn. They—always do in this kind of story." Plot, the be-all and end-all of adventure movies, is undermined by irony. Thus when, incited by Beau, the defenders of the fort pour out of the main gate, Feldman the scriptwriter, in the role of Digby Geste, protests frantically, "Fellers, you can't just desert! You'll miss the rest of the story!" The effect is the same when a printed explanation situates the meeting between the Sheikh and Gen. Pecheur "in another part of the story."

Riding away from Fort Zindeneuf, the Sheikh meets Rudolph Valentino—not the real one (even though the grainy, scratched texture of the film suggests we are looking at an old black-and-white print) but a false Valentino, played by Martin Snaric with whom he heads for an illuminated city of illusion, while the orchestra plays *Hollywood*. Time after time, *The Last Remake* offers a reminder that Surrealists consider salutary, showing film to be the medium of illusion. When the nipples on a portrait of Queen Victoria at Geste Manor are manipulated, the picture opens down the middle to reveal a safe. The shade Markov and Boldini pull down for privacy while they are plotting bears a painting depicting the very sentry they want to shut out of sight. Before working further through the *Kama Sutra*, Gen. Pecheur discreetly turns to the wall a portrait of Emperor Napoleon (his right hand inserted in the front of his pants, not his tunic): the reverse of the picture displays a back view of Bonaparte. A legionnaire's arm falls off, after being released by a wounded comrade who has supported it in the salute position, in response to the order "Present arms!" The mirror Boldini holds while cutting Markov's hair still reflects the sergeant's face, when held up behind his head.

Shown to the accompaniment of *Rule Britannia*, a shot of a fort in the sand is juxtaposed with footage of dancing legionnaires who are complying with Markov's strict order to enjoy themselves. The spectator naturally infers that the soldiers are inside the fort. But a passing horse's hoof destroys the structure. As the camera pans right, we see a child's pail on which a saluting toy soldier is painted and we realize we have been looking at a sandcastle, for no identifiable reason built in the Sahara. After Digby has commented sadly that Beau and Flavia "would never have made their way through that *parched* desert," a burning sun fills the screen and we hear:

FLAVIA: "Oh darling, if I should die now, I would die happy, [we see her head next to Beau's] happy in your arms."
BEAU: "Oh, Mother!"
FLAVIA: "If it were not for this thirst, this damned thirst."

The sound of seagulls makes itself heard and Beau sits up on a beach to ask a waiter to bring champagne, "extremely well iced."

Technically, as well as thematically, *The Last Remake of Beau Geste* deals in illusions. No expense has been spared in producing this film. It evidently has escaped budgetary restrictions that, by and large, have stood between the Surrealists and making films uncontaminated by commercialism. Yet its director points with self-mockery to the source of his funds. He interrupts the battle sequence in the desert, freezing the film on a shot of Digby Geste being prodded in the backside by a warrier's lance, so that a professional salesman (Ed McMahon, dressed up as a tribesman) can introduce a commercial for used camels.

Repeatedly Marty Feldman avails himself of the competent services of Albert Whitlock (special visual effects) and John Stears (special effects supervisor), not to bolster the illusion of reality through film but to attack it. Specifically cinematic qualities contribute to deriding realism in his movie, in this way coincidentally preparing Surrealism's infiltration of the world of conventional film reality.

Digby's assisted escape from one of Her Majesty's Prisons occurs during an intercut. We see a Universal one-reel silent comedy titled *The Escape*, running at accelerated speed in anachronistic black and white. The impression created bears comparison with the one obtained by Max Ernst in his Surrealist *collage*-novels through incorporation of incongruous material culled from old prints and turn-of-the-century book illustrations. Technically, unification of narrative truth and fancy is achieved on the visual plane with noteworthy skill, in another scene which, nevertheless, Feldman takes care to set off from his film as obviously the product of undeniable illusion.

Lagging behind the column on the march to Fort Zindeneuf, Digby notices a large billboard, visible to none of the other soliders, apparently. It gives clear warning: "Caution. You are entering Mirage Area." Here a Paramount Picture, Wellman's *Beau Geste*, invades the screen. In a short black-and-white sequence, Digby-Marty Feldman converses with Beau-Gary Cooper, seated across the table from him:

BEAU-COOPER: "Digby, somebody *always* gets out of these things. It might be *you*."

DIGBY-FELDMAN: "I bloody well hope it is! Look, can you just direct me to the end of this scene? That's all I ask."

Cooper hands him a cigarette and Digby discovers why this man he recognizes as someone he has seen in the movies always talks so slowly: "Moroccan gold, eh! Legion issue.... Really heavy shit, Big G!" The mirage comes to a close when, jumping through a black-and-white screen image ("The End"), Digby returns to the Technicolor world of the remake, leaving the whole episode neatly framed between the first billboard and the second, inscribed, "You have just left Mirage Area."

If any one sequence may be cited as summing up *The Last Remake of Beau Geste* it is this one. The brief scene is completely faithful to the spirit of iconoclasm in which Feldman's movie treats myths. It turns healthy vulgarity to account in reducing modern mythology to shreds. More than this, it demonstrates that noteworthy technical sophistication in the movies can be a potent means of stressing the fragility of the very illusion we are accustomed to see film-makers conscientiously labor to create and maintain in the cinema. In these important respects, *The Last Remake* must impress the Surrealist as no less consistent with his idea of cinema than the moral posture it reflects is, to his mind, exemplary.

9

Conclusion

IN HIS *Le Surréalisme au cinéma* (1963) Ado Kyrou offers a passing comment on *The Enchanted Cottage*. While doing so, he ascribes this film to one of the coauthors of the screenplay, Herman T. Mankiewicz, without mentioning the other, De-Witt Bodeen, or the director, and neglecting to point out that the script is an adaptation of a stage play by a popular English dramatist, Arthur Pinero. Pronouncing the movie "admirable," Kyrou goes on to summarize it in these terms: "A disfigured man and an ugly girl are transformed by a love that will unite them beyond all ugliness and it is a handsome couple that will leave the dwelling-place" (p. 129). This is to say that he seriously misrepresents the subject matter of *The Enchanted Cottage*, in which two people in love see one another as beautiful without actually undergoing a physical change perceptible to anyone else. Meanwhile, bent on opposing Henri Agel's interpretation of John Cromwell's movie as spiritual, in *Amour-Erotisme et cinéma* (1966) Kyrou simply ignores a perfectly clear statement by the couple's blind confidant: "Take this gift and enjoy it, without question, without fear. Accept it humbly, as a heaven-sent miracle and be grateful for it. . . . You've both been touched by a power that is beyond this world. Accept your blessing."

It is true that *The Enchanted Cottage* is marked by some ambiguity. It presents a gift from heaven as unquestionably carnal in nature, communicating the impression that love thrives best on physical attraction. Moreover, when the couple discover that they are not changed after all in other people's eyes, Oliver refers to his and Laura's ugliness as "the truth about us." Their landlady, who has worked as their house-keeper, explains, "You've fallen in love. And a man and

185

woman in love have a gift of sight that isn't granted other people.... Keep your love burning, keep it burning and I promise you'll never be anything to one another but fair and handsome. *That*'s the charm. That's the secret of the only enchantment the cottage holds and it's of your own making." Yet this explanation (flatly contradicting the other we have just heard), by a woman who confesses to having observed no change in the young couple, leads only to triteness. Oliver's observation, "You'll always be beautiful to me" elicits from Laura the equally hackneyed reply, "And nothing could ever change the way I feel about you. You know that."

The Enchanted Cottage seems to end in sentimental banality because the above extracts from the screenplay conceal from us the most impressive contribution made by filming to the themes of Pinero's play. The movie lets us *see* love wipe away the scars on a wounded flyer's face and soften the lines on his wife's. More important still, we are shown that, transformed by love, Oliver is able to use his crippled right arm even though, in the presence of others, it hangs useless so that he cannot even embrace his mother at the moment when he expects her to notice how changed he is since marrying Laura.

Of course, there is ambiguity here, too, an indecisiveness that makes interpretation a speculative venture. As we hear the words of love reproduced above, the couple's facial features are indistinguishable against the light from the window. Oliver, though, has to use his serviceable left hand to scratch his name on the pane next to those of lovers who have resided in the cottage previously. All the same, we in the audience find ourselves implicated as witnesses in a situation more complex by far than that of strictly visual illusion in which a friend who, being blind, cannot see the lovers and judges them to be "playing a part" even though, he admits, they do not know it.

At the end of the movie, as Oliver and Laura are about to enter a house where guests will be able to observe his disfigurement and her sadly plain features, they pause to look at one another. For the last time before the final fade-out, we are privileged to see them as they see one another and as others in the film cannot see them. We are granted visual proof of the enchantment of the cottage where they fell in love. We are shown that this enchantment is maintained by their continuing devotion to one another. Presumably it will keep them beautiful in each other's eyes as long as they live. On balance, therefore, the source of this precious gift is less important than the fact that it is theirs to enjoy.

This brings us to another important fact, that Ado Kyrou is capable of seeing and hearing only what he wants to in the work of a film-maker whose existence he ignores. What Cromwell may have meant to demonstrate through his story of the beautifying consequences of love does not really matter to a Surrealist. Kyrou practices his habitual selectivity in responding to the movie passing before his eyes, entirely free of any sense of obligation to take account of the director's purpose, stated or presumed, wherever doing so might conflict with his own viewpoint. While we may speak of distortion with regard to his account of *The Enchanted Cottage*, we should be unfair to attribute it to conscious intent, aimed at imposing on the narrative material of a movie a pattern meant to break with the interpretation it provides of love's role in human life. Although failure to show good faith seems to be the main issue as we review Kyrou's version of what goes on in Cromwell's film, this is not really the case. For Kyrou keeps faith with Surrealism when setting down recollections of a Hollywood movie seen possibly no more than once, after they have been filtered through a sensibility indelibly marked by Surrealist aspirations.

Few people indeed would subscribe to Kyrou's argument, on the very first page of *Le Surréalisme et cinéma*, that cinema is Surrealist in essence. Even so, looking over the available evidence, no objective observer can deny that Surrealism is capable of illuminating certain films produced entirely outside its influence. By the same token, in the right circumstances cinema lends itself to shedding light on Surrealism. For it can bring to the surface characteristics of the Surrealist sensibility to which the unique qualities of film have the special virtue of being able to direct attention.

When in a note on Mae Murray published in *Littérature* (March 1922), Jacques Rigaut exclaimed, "Drugs dispense with justification," he alluded to the Surrealist approach to film in a manner that could seem quite confusing, if the drug of cinema were to be considered a palliative. In reality, for

Surrealists movies are a stimulant, "a remarkable stimulant," as Artaud called them, "a stimulant capable of peopling our deserted nights," as Desnos put it in *Paris-Journal* on April 27, 1923. Moreover, the manner in which films stimulate the Surrealist is enlightening.

Film is a mode of expression that, beyond the practical limitations to which theater traditionally submits, appeals at the same time to eye and ear, to mind and imagination. Thus its particular value lies not simply in managing to satisfy Surrealist demands but also in clarifying these. It gives the Surrealist what he wants, while concurrently assisting him in establishing what his needs really are. To a Surrealist like Breton, or Kyrou, or Brunius, the lyrical quality of a film is actually less often intrinsic, we are entitled to infer, than extrinsic. It is a quality furnished mainly by the spectator himself. Looking at this or that Hollywood film, Surrealists call upon their own imaginative resources to contribute significantly to the *"power to disorient"* ascribed to the medium of cinema in Breton's 1947 essay *"Comme dans un bois."* This is their way of participating actively and profitably in the celebration of an *"absolutely modern* mystery," identified with film-viewing when Breton draws a quite surprising parallel between moviegoing and church attendance.

Upon reflection it appears that the "mystery" to which Breton pointedly refers does not bring to mind at all the kind of community of faith suggested by his parallel. In fact, participating on their own terms, Surrealists often enough find themselves responding according to their own beliefs and aspirations, instead of sharing in the experience to which the movie invites us. This is the odd thing about *"Comme dans un bois."* Having established a questionable comparison, it goes on to emphasize what weakens the parallel.

Breton speaks without equivocation of *"going beyond"* the stage of "the permitted" in the direction of "the forbidden." In the process, he demonstrates that, where film is concerned, this procedure entails following a distinctive orientation in thought and feeling no less than it does glad surrender to the attractions of film per se. What is more, the vocabulary used in *"Comme dans un bois"* leaves no doubt on one score. Expansion of a movie through the "mystery" of which Breton speaks can entail—seems in fact to positively require—violation of the material in question. At all events, it contravenes the agreement according to which film-makers bring their work before the public and claim attention.

Interestingly, André Breton sees no reason to conceal this fact. He even goes so far as to confide that, at one period of his life, in the direction of "increasing disorientation" he sought what he termed "delectation" in "the most wretched cinematographic productions." He points this out, we may assume, in order to bring to our notice the stress he placed at that time on the greatest possible "intentional discordance" between what some movie had to offer (its "lesson," as he terms it) and the spectator's natural predispositions.

Our first response to such an attitude is to condemn it as a sign of individual perverseness. We are willing enough to regard it as enlightening Breton's peculiar temperament. But apparently it is to be granted no special significance in connection with the reaction to cinema manifested by Surrealists in general. Nevertheless, the fact that Breton troubled himself to go see movies he knew would clash with his own predispositions, even making a special effort to seek these out, is worthy of notice.

For one thing, Breton's approach to movie-watching takes experimentation with film-viewing out of the realm of haphazard juxtaposition of unrelated cinematic images, such as he and Jacques Vaché had practiced in Nantes no later than 1916, before Surrealism was born. It is not enough, any longer, to avoid acquaintance with the name of the film playing before one decides to enter a movie house, and of leaving at the first twinge of boredom to head for another theater and then, quite soon, for still another. No less important, Breton highlights the nature of the exercise (the word seems quite apt) in which he now indulged. Deliberately selecting material that looked unpromising, he would approach it with the avowed purpose of submitting it to an interpretive procedure in full accord with Surrealism's fundamental principles. This is to say, he aimed at defeating the objective by means of the subjective. His aim was to extend to the cinema the poetic process that Péret called "a rectification of the universe," by which the world is to be brought into line with ideals and desires that give Surrealists their reason for living. He no longer expected simply to leave the theater "charged"—to use his own word—by an experience in which one shares quite passively. Instead, adopting an active posture, he imposed on unprepossessing movie material a value that only the intervention of his own imagination could give it.

The line of conduct sketched in Breton's *"Comme dans un bois"* is no less extreme, among Surrealists, than Philippe Soupault's short-lived habit of going to the movies daily. It is none the less valuable in helping focus our attention on the state of mind in which Surrealists watch films, as though cinema can be expected to measure up all the time to standards that commercialism really makes no attempt at all to meet. Just as valuable is a little-known event in the history of Surrealism's relations with the movie medium.

Early in 1968 a film club called L'Age d'Or was formed in the French provincial town of Rouen. Between 1968 and the summer of 1970 when it closed its doors, the club had three hundred sixty members It remains a unique experiment about which its initiator, Aurélien Dauguet, has this to say:

L'AGE D'OR film club was born of the rather ambitious desire to see the surrealist idea of cinematic expression shared by means of a didactic instrument, on the levels of poetry, sensibility and politics. It was a difficult task, because it did not mean considering, in the history of cinematographic art, only authentically surrealist works but also showing films that, from one aspect or another, were capable of illustrating and nourishing the surrealist sense of life. This is why the L'AGE D'OR Film Club aimed more at illustrating POETRY, LOVE, LIBERTY in the movies than surrealist cinema per se.[1]

The same three key-words of Surrealist faith appear in a manifesto Dauguet published anonymously when founding his club. Under the title *Lanterne magique*, the manifesto predictably attacked established forms of cinema, from French movie comedy to "the insipid soup of Hollywood tinsel." More than this, it promised that attention would go not only to movies made by Surrealists but also to "films for which the only criterion is that they can be projected with the same incandescence both wherever people are fighting for the liberation of man and on the body of the woman one loves."

Distractingly fanciful though the latter part of Dauguet's statement may sound, the import of his message is clear. Noticeably, as with Breton's remarks in *"Comme dans un bois,"* stress falls on mental and emotional preconditioning colored by political conviction, without which, over the years, the Surrealists' reaction to cinema would not have presented the remarkable consistency with which it has always been marked.

Looking over the kind of commentary that Surrealists have had to offer on film, we find it to be singularly lacking in balance, unfairly weighted in favor of some aspects of movie production and just as unfair to others. It seems that all Surrealists tend to share Ado Kyrou's knack for missing what he does not choose to see and for passing over whatever he prefers not to know or to acknowledge. For instance, when praising *Peter Ibbetson* none of these men and women, so critical of the pernicious influence of stage on cinema, feels constrained to take into account that Henry Hathaway brought George du Maurier's novel to the screen by way of a stage adaptation by Nathanael Raphael. As for Joseph von Sternberg's *Shanghai Gesture*, not one of those who have commented on this movie from the vantage point of Surrealism has bothered to analyze in detail the supposed virtues of the film over the Broadway play upon which it is based.

It is significant that when Kyrou contends that cinema is Surrealist in essence he admits only tacitly that his evaluation applies on the plane of technology. No Surrealist, it is true, has ever denied in so many words that there is a cinematic way of telling a story. Yet such is the Surrealists' fear of the negative effects of technical sophistication in any creative medium that, with regard to the movies, they have demonstrated little sensitivity to even the most obvious advantages of an expressive mode to which, nevertheless, they ascribe the greatest potential for poetic communication. Instead, they have bemoaned studied technique, which they see as diverting cinema from its true course. Discussing avant-garde cinema in the magazine *Documents* in 1929, Robert Desnos grumbled, "An erroneous mode of thought attributable to the persistent influence of Oscar Wilde and the aesthetes of 1890, an influence to which we owe among other manifestations that of Mr. Jean Cocteau, has created in the cinema a baleful confusion." Kyrou takes up the same theme in *Le Surréalisme au cinéma* where, voicing his detestation of aristocrats and aristocracies, he declares, "They can keep their Bressons and their Cocteaus" (p. 90). As for André Breton, he never deviated from the judgment he passed on Cocteau in a letter to Tristan Tzara written December 26, 1919: "My feeling, quite disinterested I swear, is that he is the most hateful person of our time."[2]

It is easy to lose sight of essentials, as issues appear clouded by personal antipathy. Hence Breton's condemnation of Cocteau needs to be examined next to Philippe Soupault's. Almost forty years after his exclusion from the Surrealist group, Soupault was to remark, "But it must be acknowledged that unfortunately Surrealism has been somewhat deformed by those who wished to make use of it rather than be of use to it, and I'm thinking in particular of a man I consider a cheat, a 'trickster', that is, Jean Cocteau."[3] It is not Cocteau, the man, whom Surrealists detest but what he stands for in cinema. Thus in his *En Marge du cinéma français* (1954), Jacques B. Brunius deplored in movies "the triumph of craftsmanship over imagination," of "procedure" over "true imagination," asserting that "tricks never replace poetry" (p. 181).

It was Brunius's belief that everything that Surrealists look to the movies to provide has been sacrificed in an industry whose development he himself, writing in 1947, associated with senility, not with increasing maturity. By and large, indeed, it seems perfectly just to condemn the commercial cinema in America on the grounds specified by Brunius. And even the criticisms summarized by Benjamin Péret have a bearing on the situation: "In other respects, the artists who have chosen to express themselves through cinema (I mean by that the script writers and directors, not the actors whose role remains secondary) run into capital which asks of them before anything else, 'How much of a return will I get on my money?' As long as this situation goes unchanged, the cinema will be condemned to silliness, aggravated even more by an anachronistic censorship, hedged about by prejudices with an odious Christian stink."[4]

Even the net cast so wide by Kyrou brings in a catch that looks pitiably small, when one remembers how many commercial films have been turned out, worldwide, since the cinema became a major entertainment industry. The Hollywood feature films that have earned the Surrealists' admiration and affection are ridiculously few in number. Exclusion of noncommercial undertakings, of vanguard experiments, and of features produced outside the United States reduces even further the percentage of movies deserving to be mentioned as evidence that Surrealism has managed to leave its mark on film. All the same, the Hollywood movies that have claimed the Surrealists' attention and held their interest are among those that have done most to nourish and sustain their faith in cinema as a medium uniquely qualified to bear Surrealism's message of poetic revolt.

Notes and References

Unless otherwise indicated, the place of publication for all books in French is Paris.

Chapter One

1. "Un autre Cinéma," *Les Lèvres Nues*, 7 (December 1957), 17.

2. See the introduction, "Off at a Tangent," in Hammond's *The Shadow and Its Shadow: Surrealist Writings on Cinema* (London, 1978), p. 3.

3. Gherasim Luca, Gellu Naum, Virgil Teodorescu, Trost, *Eloge de "Malombra"* (Bucharest, 1947); *L'Age du Cinéma*, 4-5 (August-November, 1951), special Surrealism issue.

4. *En Marge du cinéma français* (1954), p. 112. A censored version of Brunius's text, written in 1947, appeared under the title "Experimental Film in France," in Roger Manvell, ed., *Experimental Film* (London, 1949), where, notably, derogatory remarks about the police are suppressed.

5. "Cinema, Instrument of Poetry" (1953), as quoted in Francisco Aranda, *Luis Buñuel: A Critical Biography* [1975] (New York, 1976), p. 275.

6. "Sorcellerie et cinéma," in his *Œuvres complètes* (1961), 3: 79-80.

7. *Le Surréalisme au cinéma* (1963), p. 271. Expanded version of a book first published in 1953.

8. *Amour-Erotisme et cinéma* (1966), p. 180. Expanded version of a book first published in 1957.

9. "Ma femme m'affame," *La Brèche: action surréaliste*, 7. (December, 1964), 81.

10. See Luis Buñuel's review of Keaton's *College* in *Cahiers d'Art*, 10, 1927. The indisputable originality evidenced in one Surrealist's article should be noted: Petr Král's study of Larry Semon in *Positif*, 106 (June, 1960), 28-33.

11. One such occasion was a talk Ray gave at a film showing at the American Contemporary Gallery, Hollywood, on October 15, 1943. It ended: "To sum up, as far as the cinema is concerned, the worst films I have seen, that is, those that put me to sleep, contain ten or fifteen minutes that are wonderful. In the same way, I may add that the best films I have seen contain only ten or fifteen minutes that are worth while. Which in no way discourages me or makes me a pessimist. I do believe that the movies will become a great art one day—when the production of a film will really be in the hands of one master-mind." (From the text sent by Man Ray to Gilbert Neiman.)

Chapter Two

1. "Du Décor," *Le Film*, September, 1918.
2. *Films*, 15 (January 15, 1924). Soupault's text was reprinted from the magazine *Littérature*, founded by him in collaboration with Aragon and Breton.
3. "Les Mystères de New York," *Le Merle*, 1929. Louis Gasnier's serial *The Exploits of Elaine* was known in France as *Les Mystères de New York*.
4. Caption appearing in Ado Kyrou's *Le Surréalisme au cinéma* (1963) beneath a still from *Singin' in the Rain*, showing Cyd Charisse dancing with Gene Kelly.
5. "Leo et les aléas." Interview published in *Cahiers du Cinéma*, 163, February, 1965.
6. "The Marx Brothers," *Cinema*, 8 (1971), 31.
7. "Les Frères Marx," *La Nouvelle Revue française*, January 1, 1932.
8. Alain and Odette Virmaux, *Les Surréalistes et le cinéma* (1976), p. 25.
9. "Printemps, surréalisme et cinéma," *L'Ecran français*, 45 (May 8, 1946).
10. *Manifestes du surréalisme* (1962), p. 49.
11. From a response by Marco Ristic to a survey opened in the first number of the Yugoslav Surrealist publication *Nadrealizam danas i ovde* on the theme, "Is Humor a Moral Attitude?"

Chapter Three

1. Quoted by Orville Goldner and George E. Turner, *The Making of King Kong* (New York, 1976), p. 37.
2. *On Photography* (New York, 1977), pp. 14-15.
3. In this sense, *King Kong* develops a theme that elicited praise from the Surrealists for Monique Watteau's *L'Ange à fourrure* (1959),

a novel about a love affair between a woman zoologist and a large monkey, one chapter of which they reprinted in their magazine *Le Surréalisme, même,* 4 (Spring, 1958), 4-11.

The doorknocker of Count Zaroff's castle in Schoedsack and Pichel's *The Most Dangerous Game* depicts a wounded centaur bearing a woman in his arms. Based on a screenplay by James A. Creelman, with music by Max Steiner, *The Most Dangerous Game* was released before *King Kong,* in 1932, but was made at the same time, with some of the same performers (Fay Wray, Robert Armstrong, Noble Johnson) and even some of the same jungle sets. It is much admired by the Surrealists as a work marked by the influence of one of their idols, the Marquis de Sade.

    4. "King-Kong," *Minotaure,* 5 (1934), 5.
    5. *Manifestes du surréalisme* (1962), p. 22.

Chapter Four

    1. Kyrou condemns this film as "abominably imperialist," in *Amour-Erotisme et cinéma.* One must suppose him unaware of the fact that the director originally assigned to *Lives of a Bengal Lancer* was Ernest B. Schoedsack. Hathaway completed the movie after Schoedsack had left Paramount to join Cooper at RKO. At Paramount, incidentally, Cooper and Schoedsack had not baulked at producing and directing (in 1929) a film hardly less imperialist: a version of A. E. W. Mason's novel *The Four Feathers,* in which the role of Ethne was played by Fay Wray.

    2. "Le Rossignol ne se laisse pas nourrir de fables," *Cahiers G.L.M.* (1938), p. 119. This seventh number of the *Cahiers G.L.M.* is a special issue devoted to texts and illustrations on the theme of dreaming, assembled by André Breton.

    3. "Dans les eaux du rêve et le feu de l'action," *Cahiers G.L.M.* (1938), p. 94.

    4. Georges Hugnet, "Les Revenants futurs," *Cahiers G.L.M.* (1938), p. 100.

    5. Pierre Mabille, "Sur la scène du rêve," *Cahiers G.L.M.* (1938), p. 83.

    6. See the text published by Lise Deharme in *St. Cinéma des prés,* 1, 1949.

    7. P. 27. This lexicon appeared, without author's name, in a series, "Le Désordre," edited by the Surrealist Jean Schuster. All contributors to the volume were, at the time of its appearance, participants in the Surrealist movement. The entry "Eroticism" appears anonymously.

    8. *Lexique succinct de l'érotisme,* p. 75. Entry signed by Yves Elléoët, André Breton's son-in-law.

9. *Ibid.*, p. 67. Entry signed by Nora Mitrani.
10. "Contre le cinéma commercial," *L'Age du Cinéma*, 1, 1951.

Chapter Five

1. *Manifestes du surréalisme* (1962), p. 29.
2. Jehan Mayoux, "André Breton et le surréalisme," *Contre-Courant*, 143, dated "beginning of December 1966," no pagination.
3. *Arcane 17* enté d'*Ajours* (1947), p. 167. *Arcane 17* first appeared in France the year *Dark Passage* was released.
4. *Le Déshonneur des poètes* (n.d.), p. 75. Originally published in Mexico City in 1945.
5. "La Pensée est UNE et indivisible," *VVV*, 4 (February, 1944), 10.
6. *La Peinture au défi*, catalogue of an exhibition of *collages*, held in Paris at the Galerie Goemans in 1929-1930. The catalogue was published in 1930 and is reprinted in Aragon's *Les Collages* (1965), pp. 35-71.
7. *Anthologie de l'Amour sublime* (1956), p. 137. The fact that Péret was an active militant revolutionary lends weight to his stress on the antisocial aspects of love.

Chapter Six

1. *Etudes cinématographiques*, 40-42 (1965), 168.
2. Quoted in Jacques Doniol-Valcrose and André Bazin, "Entretiens avec Luis Buñuel," *Cahiers du Cinéma*, 36 (June 1954).
3. *Manifestes du surréalisme* (1962), p. 28.

Chapter Seven

1. See Mandiargues, "The Pommeraye Arcade," in J. H. Matthews, ed., *The Custom-House of Desire: a Half-Century of Surrealist Short Stories* (Berkeley, Los Angeles, London, 1975), 267-79.
2. *Manifestes du surréalisme* (1962), p. 27.
3. The quotations appearing here are taken from the soundtrack of *The Night of the Hunter* where the dialogue differs in numerous small details from the text of Agee's film-play as printed in *Agee on Film*, Vol. 2 (New York, 1969).
4. *Dorothy and Lillian Gish by Lillian Gish* (New York, 1973), p. 255. François Truffaut, whose reservations about *The Night of the Hunter* are typical of those expressed by movie critics, made a bid for originality in his 1956 review of the film when he asserted, "All the

characters are good, even the apparently evil preacher." See his *The Films in My Life* (New York, 1978), p. 120.

5. Heroism is the theme in Agee's other major film-plays, *The African Queen* and *Noa Noa* (based on the life of Gauguin) which was never filmed.

Chapter Eight

1. See Jacques B. Brunius, "The Goon Show," *Le Surréalisme, même*, 2 (1957), 86-88. When Sir Hector Geste says, "Damn and blast my wife, God bless her," Crumble adds, "and all who sail in her!" This kind of thought association was practiced countless times in the *Goon Show* scripts. See J. H. Matthews, *Toward the Poetics of Surrealism* (Syracuse, N.Y., 1976), 189-204.

2. The words of the Legion song audible as the movie opens run:

> We'll give our all for France.
> We'll break our bones for France.
> . . . .
> We'll lose our legs or at least an eye
> With great panache
> For France and a little more hash, hash, hash, hash.
> We're all for one, for France.
> To die is fun, for France.
> We'll torture and maim, we will kill and be killed
> For glory and fame, we are really thrilled.
> . . . .
> So bring on the Arabs with sabres and knives.
> We'll murder the men and we'll rape all their wives
> For Liberty, Freedom, Nobility, Money.
> And then, perhaps for a change,
> We'll murder the wives and rape all the men
> For France, for France.

3. A man's got to be
> What a man's got to be.
> He must look his heart right in the eye
> Without flinching to see.
> He must be what he must.
> He must *must* what he be
> Just to be what he was
> What he will be because
> He will be what he is.
> A man's got to do
> What a man's got to do.
> He must ask himself who
> Am I, when am I, why am I now that I'm who?
> And what am I when?
> And when am I what?

And why aren't I who I am when I am what I am
When I am not?
Oh what is a hero but a man who's no choice?
He needs courage and guts and long wavy hair,
A high tenor voice.
He must climb the impossible dream and then,
With a lump in his throat,
He must try with his last ounce of courage
to reach the impossible note!

Chapter Nine

1. Letter to the author, April 27, 1978.
2. Letter reproduced in Michel Sanouillet, *Dada à Paris* (1965), p 454.
3. See the interview granted Jean-Marie Mabire in *Etudes cinématographiques*, 38-39 (1965), 31.
4. "Contre le cinéma commercial," *L'Age du Cinéma*, 1 (1951).

Selected Bibliography

Books by Surrealists

ARTAUD, ANTONIN. *Œuvres complètes*, Vol. 3. Paris: Gallimard, 1961. Brings together Artaud's film scenarios — Surrealist and postSurrealist — as well as his essays on cinema.

BENAYOUN, ROBERT. *Le Dessin animé après Walt Disney*. Paris: Pauvert, 1961. With chapters on Norman McLaren and Tex Avery, as well as European film-makers, this standard work on animated film renders further study of cartoons, considered from the Surrealist viewpoint, redundant.

BRUNIUS, JACQUES B. *En Marge du cinéma français*. Paris: Arcanes, 1954. Written in 1947 and first published, with some cuts, in English translation (Roger Manvell, ed., *Experimental Film*, London; Grey Walls Press, 1949), this essay by a Surrealist moviemaker and theoretician of film makes a plea for a marginal experimental cinema, freed of the aesthetic restraints of the French avant-garde.

DESNOS, ROBERT. *Cinéma*. Paris: Gallimard, 1966. Besides Desnos's film scenarios, this collection assembles the writings of a man who worked as a professional film critic and was expelled from the Surrealist group for the crime of journalism.

HAMMOND, PAUL. *The Shadow and Its Shadow: Surrealist Writings on Cinema*. London: British Film Institute, 1978. A collection of important Surrealist texts in English translation, prefaced by an essay, "Off at a Tangent," written from the Surrealist standpoint.

KYROU, ADO. *Amour-Erotisme et cinéma*. Paris: Le Terrain Vague, 1957, reprinted 1966. Written from the Surrealist perspective, this study of the theme of love in movies presents the same characteristics as its author's *Le Surrealisme au cinema*.

——. *Le Surréalisme au cinéma*. Paris: Arcanes, 1953; Revised edition, Paris: Le Terrain Vague, 1963. The later edition is a somewhat expanded version of a highly subjective study of the manifestation of the Surrealist spirit in the international cinema, of-

201

fered without the preface contributed to the original by the Surrealist Jean Ferry.

Critical Studies

MATTHEWS, J. H. *Surrealism and Film*. Ann Arbor: University of Michigan Press, 1971. Discusses Surrealism and the commercial cinema, Surrealist film scripts, Surrealist film-makers, and Luis Buñuel, "the surrealist as commercial director."

MITRY, JEAN. *Le Cinéma expérimental*. Paris: Seghers, 1974. Has three pertinent chapters: "Surréalisme et cinema," "Surréalisme U.S.A.," and "Séquelles du surréalisme."

RONDOLINO, GIANNI. *L'Occhio tagliato*. Turin: Martano, 1972. A collection of Dada and Surrealist texts, reproduced for the most part in French.

VIRMAUX, ALAIN and ODETTE. *Les Surréalistes et le cinéma*. Paris: Seghers, 1976. One-third of this volume is devoted to arguing that Surrealism failed in the cinema; the remainder is given over to reproductions of writings relating to cinema by Surrealists and their critics.

Special Numbers of Magazines

L'Age du Cinéma, No. 4-5, August-November, 1951.
Etudes cinématographiques, Nos. 38-39 and 40-42, 1965.

Filmography

DARK PASSAGE (Warner Bros.-First National, 1947).
Producer: Jerry Wald.
Director: Delmer Daves.
Screenplay: Delmer Daves, from the novel by David Goodis.
Cinematographer: Sid Hickox.
Special Effects: H. F. Koenenkamp.
Costumes: Bernard Newman.
Music: Frank Waxman.
Sound: Dolph Thomas.
Editor: David Weisbart.
Cast: Humphrey Bogart (Vincent Parry), Lauren Bacall (Irene Jansen), Agnes Moorehead (Madge Rapf), Bruce Bennett (Bob), Tom D'Andrea (Sam the cabby), Clifton Young (Baker), Rory Mallinson (George Fallsinger).
Running Time: 106 minutes.
Première: September 1947
16mm. Rental: United Artists

DUCK SOUP (Paramount, 1933).
Director: Leo McCarey.
Screenplay: Bert Kalmar and Harry Ruby (with additional dialogue by Arthur Sheekman and Nat Perrin).
Cinematographer: Henry Sharp.
Art Directors: Hans Dreier and Wiard B. Ihnen.
Music: Bert Kalmar and Harry Ruby.
Music Direction: Arthur Johnston.
Editor: LeRoy Stone.
Cast: Groucho Marx (Rufus T. Firefly), Harpo Marx (Pinkie), Chico Marx (Chicolini), Zeppo Marx (Bob Rolland), Margaret Dumont (Mrs. Teasdale), Louis Calhern (Ambassador Trentino), Raquel Torres (Vera Marcal).
Running Time: 70 minutes.

Première: November 17, 1933.
16mm. Rental: Universal / TWYMAN.

KING KONG (RKO-Radio Pictures, 1933).
Producers / Directors: Merian C. Cooper and Ernest B. Schoedsack.
Screenplay: James A. Creelman and Ruth Rose.
Cinematographers: Eddie Lindon, Vernon Walker, J. O. Taylor.
Optical Photography: Linwood G. Dunn and William Ulm.
Chief Technician: Willis H. O'Brien.
Art Technicians: Mario Larrinaga and Byron L. Crabbe.
Sound Effects: Murray Spivack; Walter G. Elliott, associate.
Recorded by: E. A. Wolcott.
Music: Max Steiner.
Special Effects: Harry Redmond, Jr.
Set Decorations: Thomas Little.
Editor: Ted Cheesman.
Cast: Fay Wray (Ann Darrow), Robert Armstrong (Carl Denham), Bruce Cabot (John Driscoll), Frank Reicher (Captain Englehorn), Noble Johnson (Native Chief), Victor Wong (Charley), Merian C. Cooper (Flight Commander), Ernest B. Schoedsack (Chief Observer).
Running Time: 100 minutes.
Première: The film opened at the Radio City Music Hall and the New Roxy on March 2, 1933. The official première in Hollywood was at Grauman's Chinese Theatre, March 24, 1933.
16mm. Rental: Films, Inc.

THE LAST REMAKE OF BEAU GESTE (Universal Pictures, 1977).
Producer: William S. Gilmore.
Director: Marty Feldman.
First Assistant Director: Tom Joyner.
Screenplay: Marty Feldman and Chris Allen.
Cinematographer: Gerry Fisher.
Art Director: Les Dilley.
Costumes: Mary Routh.
Music: John Morris.
Sound: Peter Sutton and Kevin F. Cleary.
Sound Effects: Anthony Magro.
Editors: Jim Clark and Arthur Schmidt.
Special Visual Effects: Albert Whitlock.
Special Effects Supervisor: John Stears.
Cast: Ann-Margret (Flavia Geste), Marty Feldman (Digby Geste), Michael York (Beau Geste), Peter Ustinov (Sgt. Markov), James Earl Jones (The Sheikh), Trevor Howard (Sir Hector Geste), Special Guest Star: Gary Cooper.

Running Time: 85 minutes.
Première: July 1977.

THE NIGHT OF THE HUNTER (United Artists, 1955).
Producer: Paul Gregory.
Director: Charles Laughton.
Assistant Director: Milton Carter.
Screenplay: James Agee, from the novel by Davis Grubb.
Cinematographer: Stanley Cortez.
Art Director: Hilyard Brown.
Music: Walter Schumann.
Sound: Stanford Naughton.
Editor: Robert Golden.
Cast: Robert Mitchum (Harry Powell), Shelley Winters (Willa Harper), Lillian Gish (Rachel Cooper), Billy Chapin (John Harper), Sally Jane Bruce (Pearl Harper), Evelyn Varden (Icey Spoon), Don Beddoe (Walt Spoon), Peter Graves (Ben Harper).
Running time: 91 minutes.
Première: September, 1955.
16mm. Rental: United Artists.

PANDORA AND THE FLYING DUTCHMAN (A Dorkay / Romulus Production, released by Independent Film Distributors, 1951).
Producer / Director: Albert Lewin.
Screenplay: Albert Lewin.
Cinematographer: Jack Cardiff.
Art Director: John Bryan.
Music: Alan Rawsthorne.
Editor: Ralph Kemplin.
Cast: James Mason (Hendrick van der Zee), Ava Gardner (Pandora Reynolds), Nigel Patrick (Stephen Cameron), Mario Cabre (Juan Montalvo).
Running Time: 122 minutes.
Première: November, 1951.
16mm. Rental: Not currently available.

PETER IBBETSON (Paramount, 1935).
Producer: Louis D. Lighton.
Director: Henry Hathaway.
Screenplay: Constance Collier, Vincent Lawrence, Waldemar Young, John Meehan, Edwin Justus Mayer, from the novel by George du Maurier, adapted for the stage by Nathaniel Raphael.
Cinematographer: Charles Lang.
Art Directors: Hans Dreier and Robert Usher.
Music: Ernest Toch.

Sound: Harry D. Mills.
Editor: Stuart Heisler.
Cast: Gary Cooper (Peter Ibbetson), Ann Harding (Mary, Duchess of
    Towers), John Halliday (Duke of Towers), Virginia Weidler
    (Mimsey), Dickie Moore (Gogo [Pierre]).
Running Time: 85 minutes.
Première: New York opening at the Radio City Music Hall,
    November 7, 1935.
16mm. Rental: Universal 16.

Index

207